THE MAGIC OF
SCRUB HOLLER

A rich and rewarding collection of Ozark Mountain life.

BY LANNY GIBSON

Illustrations by Derlyne Gibson

To Betty

Best Wishes from

Scrub Holler

Lanny

9/11/04

The Magic of Scrub Holler

by

Lanny Gibson

ISBN 0-9717725-0-9

ACKNOWLEDGEMENTS

The author wishes to thank the following magazines and newspapers in which the stories in this collection were originally published:

Arkansas Times Magazine

Berryville Star-Progress

Eureka Springs Times-Echo

Green Forest Tribune

Holiday Island Regional News

Journal of Carroll County

FOREWORD

About a decade ago I came across a clearly unusual school-teacher in a small Ozark mountain town called Berryville. Well, Lanny's not quite unusual. He's special, like a honey moth or a redbud tree — sometimes he can be a chigger. He was an English teacher for a living, but his real life was his farm on Ford Mountain, called Scrub Holler and various other appellations depending on his mood. Over the years as I came to know him better through his submissions to my newspaper, I recognized his demeanor as that of an artist with a deep intelligence, maybe genius, who loved writing and farming so much that his stories reflected a singular and dedicated mind that could embrace the treasure of life on the farm, and the farm's cold shoulder to the human life it sustained and depended upon .

His dry humor and wild imagination were a joy to experience.

His talent for capturing life on the farm with warmth, humor and insight transfixed the readers of four small newspapers in his farming community, and he spent a dozen years recording oral histories of the good old boys and gals who would stand around the tailgate of a battered pickup, talking tall tales and true tales of woe and wonder.

As the cover of this book suggests, it is not about farming. It is about life. It is about the magic of Scrub Holler and the magic of a newborn calf — the knowledge of life that a farming community possesses but rarely reveals to the outside world.

There just ain't too many farmers who can write as well or spin a tale as tricky as Lanny Gibson. Dear reader, press ahead through this little book about large lives lived so quietly — it'll make you laugh and wonder at The Magic of Scrub Holler.

• Ken O'Toole, July 2001, Berryville, Arkansas

"GIBSON'S FARM'S GROWED UP"

My farm is Arkansas scrub: steep hillsides sliding off into deep hollers, knee-high stumps hiding in golden brown broom sage, rocky fields, sagging fences, weeds. Vintage Ozark Mountain Country it ain't. No matter what I do, other farmers spitting tobacco juice drive by to look. It makes their day telling their neighbors: "Gibson's farm's growed up worse'n anybody's."

I go to the feed store, the sale barn, the hardware. They look at me like my donkey don't bray.

I want everything: I want chickens that ain't dying, cows that ain't scrawny, hogs that ain't runts, roofs that ain't leaking, goats that can't jump — but most of all I want my wife to be happy.

I'm trying everything.

Each winter I spread fertilizer laced with seed. It soaks in good with the melting snow.

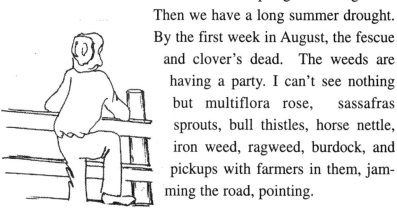

Then we have a wet spring which is good.

Then we have a long summer drought. By the first week in August, the fescue and clover's dead. The weeds are having a party. I can't see nothing but multiflora rose, sassafras sprouts, bull thistles, horse nettle, iron weed, ragweed, burdock, and pickups with farmers in them, jamming the road, pointing.

Trying to improve the pasture, I wheel my Ford tractor through the fields dragging a wagon to pick up rocks. I creep down into a deep holler to unload. When I've thrown off the last rock, I start driving the tractor up out of the holler. Its front wheels lift up off the ground on the steep incline. If I proceed, it'll rare backwards and mash me. I let it roll back.

Gently, I request my dearly beloved wife sit on the front to hold it down so I can proceed with farm improvements.

Gracefully, she climbs on. I churn up the narrow road. She notices the steep drop off beside us—I failed to tell her about that.

I deliver her safely to the level field, yet she won't allow me to help her down. Charmingly, she de-tractors and lets me have it: "You idiot! You asked me sit on the front of your tractor to hold it down— and I did! I guess you're jumping to conclusions about how much I weigh! Well, forget it. That's the last time! I don't do the front end of tractors anymore.

"You must think I'm really stupid. I could have fallen off and broken my neck, my back, my leg! I could have fallen from the tractor into that drop off you didn't tell me about!

"Besides—why did you ask me to sit up there in the first place? That must mean you already thought I was heavy enough to hold it down.

"Get out of your scaly head the idea that I am heavy! I am NOT heavy! I'm an independent woman—not a circus performer!"

After I assure her she is as light as the scent of a lily, I see a trace of the smile on her lips that directs me to dedicate myself to her happiness and to the improvement of this farm. But I know I must look for another unloading place for my many rocks if I am to make progress.

CHAPTER 1

SWINE NOTES: GETTING CURED

Raising hogs in Arkansas was not an undertaking I rooted out purposefully; nevertheless, I've been wallowing in it for ten years.

Pig farming began with a casual encounter and proceeded to multiply on me. I brought home a couple of pigs in a burlap sack. They were no bigger than puppies and just as cute and playful. I put them in my field to range. The next thing I knew they weighed three hundred pounds and I was talking boars and back fat. Soon I was addicted, getting my highs when the market was up, falling into a depression when the market went down, down, down.

A red Duroc sow named "Mama" initiated me further. With the birth of her piggies, Mama's placid disposition changed into a snorting bellicosity. I discovered that messing with Mama's piggies was best done with Mama safely penned elsewhere. Mama once crashed through a gate to get to me while I was doctoring her piggies. Somehow I found myself sitting in a window seven feet up in a barn wall that had no hand or foot holds in it, wondering dazedly how I'd managed the feat.

I've always heard pigs were very intelligent. I found this to be true, but I also found that their intelligence was not necessarily a blessing. Couple intelligence with independence and persistent curiosity, and it can prove to be what I call a negative factor. Intelligent pigs can open gates. Intelligent, independent, curious pigs can dismantle virtually anything that they can set their noses to. This is not always soothing. I look for a certain docile manageability in my livestock.

It wouldn't have occurred to me that a ride in a pickup truck would be the time for a pig to indulge in mischievous experiments, what with all the excitement of travel. Yet one veteran sow totally demolished the homemade wooden rack I was so proud of right off my pickup during the first three miles of a twenty-five mile trip to market one winter evening. She scattered those inexpensive pieces all along the highway. I didn't realize what she'd done until I stopped to gas up at the local gas station. The attendant, Hugh, chortled, "That sow jump on by herself, Lanny?"

I stepped out of the cab to see what he was talking about and the sow's eyes and my eyes met and there was no rack between. "Oh, my God!" I gasped, jumping back in the truck and turning around swiftly midst much laughter. She must have been satisfied with mortifying me, for she rode the three miles home standing majestically in the unguarded truck bed.

Intelligence is overrated, anyway. However, personality among pigs is something else. Every one of them is different. One walks with a regal step; one is always skittish. Another will turn out to be left-handed, or left-footed, whichever. She'll invariably back out of her farrowing stall the wrong way to find herself staring, bewildered, at the barn wall instead of an open gate to the watering and exercising lane.

Pigs love to have their bellies scratched and they'll lie down and roll over for more, except while they're eating. Actually, it's difficult to get a pig to stop eating for any reason. The only exception I ever found was when I tried to entice them to go somewhere they didn't want to go, using a pan of feed. Once the pigs sensed I was trying to manipulate them, I was sunk. They wouldn't eat at the Waldorf-Astoria with Boss Hog himself.

Male pigs are always rude. Let's face it: Boars are definitely chauvinistic. A boar can never get it through his head that he shouldn't always get exactly what he wants.

Pigs tend to be an amiable lot. Even aggravating and ill-mannered pigs are accepted by other pigs. Even so, there is a fairly constant exchange of nipping, biting, ramming, and pushing in a pig lot. A relationship with a pig involves more wear and tear than any creature other than another pig is willing to endure.

The thing to remember around pigs is that they can crunch black walnuts in the shell as easily as we munch popcorn. That kind of jaw power demands a degree of respect normally reserved for governors or NFL defensive tackles.

As I have said, pigs will not stop eating to talk, but they DO talk. Feeding time produces a mixture of bear-like growlings, pitiful drawn-out whines, and the high-pitched screams of the misjudged and misunderstood. If OSHA were to visit a pig lot at feeding time, every farmer in pigdom would be fined on the spot for excessive decibels and instantly clapped into earmuffs. Lord only knows what an OSHA agent would do if he ever witnessed the process of putting rings in the noses of hogs that range. The noise they make during this operation causes birds to cease singing, the barn to reverberate, and walnuts to fall from trees.

But the most captivating of all pig talk is the mother and piggy reunion. When her piggies have been spirited out of the sow's farrowing pen for their shots and then carefully replaced, mother and piggies greet each other with an enthusiastic series of delightful, love-chuckling snorts.

I wean my piggies when they're five weeks old and take them to market after eight weeks when they weigh sixty pounds. A truck load of fat feeder pigs gives me a sense of satisfaction of a job well done. Especially if my sows averaged ten pigs a litter and the market is up.

Pigs have long been praised as mortgage busters, and for me, it's worked out pretty well. I've always felt that we've had a deal, my pigs and I. I fed them whether the feed prices were up or down, gave them their vaccinations, cleaned their pens, and gave them a farm pond, shade, and clover. In return, I got truckloads of feeder pigs to sell.

But occasionally, I would have to haul off an old sow or boar and that seemed unfair. They were old friends I had been working with and talking to at feeding time twice a day for several years--I fed them grain in pans in the barn yard mornings and evenings. They were old friends who had done their best. When we got to the stockyard, they'd leave the truck and saunter amiably down the dark sawdusted alley with that familiar friendly, inquisitive air to disappear forever.

It about broke my heart every time. Maybe that's one reason I'm trying to get cured of the hog business. You can get addicted to pigs in more ways than one.

CHAPTER 2

EVERYBODY HAS AN ATTITUDE

Ford Mountain has many peaks, hollows and ridges, a few gaps and one or two passes. Go north from Berryville eleven miles on Highway 21. You'll see the mountain sitting over there west of Oak Grove, a.k.a. Sooter City.

Ford Mountain is not the Garden of Eden. The farms on Ford Mountain are bad for having sprouts and thistles. My neighbor on the West resolved to spray to get rid of his. He wanted a clean farm. He sprayed, and everything died — but it didn't stay dead. The next year it all grew back.

He sprayed a more powerful chemical. I saw him out there on hot days with his spray rig strapped over his shoulder. He sprayed hard that year and his sprouts died and never came back, but he turned into a wart with long, thick hairs growing out of him. When he died, the Environmental Protection Agency classified him as toxic waste — we couldn't bury him on Ford Mountain.

My neighbor on the East decided to brush hog. Trying to find a way and a time that would kill his brush, he set his brush hog high; he set his brush hog low. He brush hogged in the dark of the moon, brush hogged in the light of the moon, brush hogged in the Dog Days, brush hogged when the martins come in the spring, brush hogged when the ducks left in the fall, brush hogged on the equinox, brush hogged in the rain, brush hogged on his birthday, brush hogged at sunrise, brush hogged at sunset. He brush hogged, brush hogged, brush hogged. Nothing worked.

The Guinness people visited him. He made the Book of World Records for having the shortest, thickest sprouts with the toughest root systems anywhere in the world. The county agent prepared a pamphlet saying to destroy a root system like that, a farmer'd need a charge of dynamite powerful enough to destroy the entire mountain.

It was almost spring. I gazed over my ninety acres of Arkansas jungle. I saw the sprout-covered ridges and hollows making up my farm. I saw the hundreds, thousands, millions of buds waiting to explode into leaves. As far as I knew, I only had the choice of spraying and becoming a toxic wart or brush hogging and getting in Guinness. Not wanting to be stupid, I went to Harold's store in Sooter City to ask the group of friendly farmers that meet there every day were there any other choices a feller could make to get a clean place on Ford Mountain.

"GOATS!" they said.

"Goats?" I said.

"Yeah! Go ask them who has goats. Ask Roy—Betty—Tuck—Russell—Randy—Charlie—Orville—Vaughan—Delmer— they'll tell you goats eat the leaves and bark off brush and kill it. Goats'll clean your place."

So I set out to listen to the goat people to determine how I should proceed.

To Goat, or Not to Goat

"If there's ever another goat on my place," Roy Barnes said, "it better be running. I only had bad luck with goats. I got disgusted with them. I'm easy to get disgusted. I bought a bunch of Nubian milk goats. They was supposed to give two quarts a day — homogenized milk. They didn't. They all turned out bad. First of all, their teats were too short. I couldn't milk them. Then they got out. I never found them.

"You don't need milk goats on your place. Milk goats need a big, flat, smooth pasture where they can get high quality food.

"You need brush goats. Put you a goat wire around your place. It's wove different from hog wire. The webs are smaller so a goat can't get its head through.

"I had a goat that kept getting caught in the wire anyways. Every day, I heard her bleating, bleating and no matter what I was doing, I'd have to go get her out. One day, I went down to get her head out — it isn't easy— they pull back while you push forward and vicey-versy. After a hassle, I got her out. I turned to go, and that aggravation put her head right back in! I took the pruning shears I was carrying and cut her horns off.

"You got to put up wire that stands over four feet high. You got to put a barb on the bottom on each side of it so the coyotes can't dig under it and three barbs on top so the goats can't jump out and nothing can jump in.

"You need to put your goats in the shed of a night. If you don't, coyotes will eat the little ones faster than you can raise them up. I heard coyotes a-howling at night. Bunches of them, trying to get my goats. Their yipping and howling had a eerie sound."

• • •

Orville Wright said, "I had a Nazi goat herd. They were big and they were mean. My billy goats got huge. They were Gestapos.

"My goats were storm-trooper goats. They went stomping along, goose stepping through my land. They had Nazi helmets on their heads and swastika bands around their necks. The lead billy's name was Seig Heil.

"My goats were always getting out. My goats could flat-footed jump over a fence five feet high. I made it higher and they went to the posts and pole vaulted over. They walked up bent trees to get over. They crawled over ... over is what they wanted and what they got.

"I put goats in with my sheep. Goats are wilier. They warn sheep of coyotes or other danger. Goats will lead sheep. They have better eyes. They sense danger faster. But goats aren't very smart. When they get caught in a fence, they bleat, telling the coyotes right where to come to eat them up. Goats never learn their lesson.

"They're idiots. They stand around to watch another goat get killed. Goats will run from predators, but when one goes down, the rest of them stop to watch. I kept my goats over by Yocum Creek. They'd stand around in a semi-circle to watch one of their own get killed by a coyote or a wolf or a dog. I've seen them do it many a time.

"Coyotes go for the goat's throat to bring them down. Wolves ham-string them. Dogs do whatever it takes. Goats can't run very fast, and they're small. They're easier to catch than deer or rabbits.

"Get used to billies stinking. They pee on themselves. Pee is billy goat shaving lotion.

"Goats might taste good if you were starving to death.

"I locked my goats in a shed of a night at first. It wasn't hard to shovel up after them. Goats pass out their waste in pellets, like deer. After I figured out I didn't like goats, that if there's a Hell, that's where they all are, I quit doing anything to keep the coyotes from getting them. Let the coyotes have those Nazi devils.

"Goats did kill off everything as far as trees and sprouts were concerned. In a little while my fences were torn up, but my place looked like a golf course — it was clean."

• • •

Linda Ohler told me, "Goats bind to people real easy. Get goats. It's like a marriage. They'll be your favorite animal, but they're the ones you'll get the maddest at. They'll jump in your garden. You'll shoot your gun in the air or do something else to save the garden, but the goats won't jump out; they'll go through your fence.

"If you ever build a goat proof fence, it should hold water."

• • •

Charlie Finch said, "Gestation period is five months on goats. I got five goats out of one nanny last year. I get three or four billies to run with the herd for three or four weeks. Then I sell the billies.

That way I can control the kidding. Billies chase the nannies. It makes the nannies weak in the hot weather. Billies run nannies a lot.

"When the kidding time comes, I put the nannies into a pen until they have the kids and the kids are at least a month old.

"Kids can't keep up with the rest of the herd for the first three or four weeks. The herd goes off from the kids, and the Pyrenees don't tend goats away from the herd.

"No goat is a match for a coyote. Coyotes got twenty-five out of thirty yearling goats when I had them up in the pasture within sight of my house.

"I like goats. I wouldn't have them if they didn't keep my place clean, though. They're a nuisance for getting out there by the Cosmic Cavern. But they have a lot of uses. The buyers for goats at the sale barns are buying for goat meat. Goat meat is going to the big cities where minority groups are. The invasion of Kuwait sent goat meat prices up.

"In Mexico they use the blood from an unborn kid for medicine. They go after the fetus because its blood is so pure.

"Big horned goats are sent to New Jersey where city folks pay to hunt them. They don't have deer to hunt.

"There may be camels around here some day. They eat more brush than goats do. Seventy-five percent of a goat's diet is brush. Eighty-five percent of a camel's diet is brush. People in Kansas are using camels to eat brush."

• • •

Tuck Long said, "Realize a soft, cuddly dog is a killer when it gets together with other dogs. Nature does somethin' to em that causes them to kill.

"Let's say somebody's huntin' dogs are chasin' a fox. That fox'll run through your goats for protection if it can. It knows the goats will get riled up and the dogs will start chasin' them. You see em chasin' your goats and shoot the dogs — now you got a lawsuit.

"NO! I don't like goats. If you have anything, they'll chew it up. And anywhere goats has run, the cows don't do good. They give cows Lepto, which makes cows abort their calves.

"If somebody gave me a goat, I'd shoot it! If my children hauled goats in here, I'd run them and the goats off.

"Good you don't own any. I don't speak to people who own 'em. As I drive by, I don't even wave at 'em. If a person has goats, I won't even look at his place. I'd rather kiss a pig than look at a goat.

"In the Bible, it says that people will be selected by separating the sheep from the goats. That's comparing people to goats: hard-headed, unlearned animals. A goat is like an unrighteous person. Besides that, they stink. They don't have any sweat glands. A goat is the dumbest thing there is, ten-to-one dumber. You can't hit a goat in the head and learn him nothin'. That's what its head is for — to hit things.

"A goat is a species by himself. He's supposed to be in India or Africa, somewhere over there, I don't know.

"You got to have a ten-foot fence, and then they'll jump over it. I don't like a goat. No way I like goats. I've had experience with goats. They'll find more ways to die than to live.

"I've never knowed of anybody makin' any money on

goats. You'll never clear your land with goats. When the trees die, they'll fall on the goats and kill 'em. The rest of them'll get tangled up and die of starvation. In the meantime everything'll grow back.

"Billy goats are randy. There were some old men around here who weren't. A doctor in Eureka Springs, back in the '20s or early '30s, tried to transplant the reproductive glands out of some billies over to the men to get them back their youthful vim and vigor. The doctor operated in a hospital. He charged $750. Quite a sum back then. That was about a year's wages. Lots of the men said they was happy. But the medical profession run him off. The doctor went down across the Rio Grande from Del Rio and built a radio station to advertise his operation. I think they closed that down in '41. He died in 1942.

"People try things all the time to see what will happen. That's how we got to where we are today, experimenting to find out what'll work and what won't."

• • •

Russell Morris explained, "You know goats are wormy when they trail behind and cough. Get Spanish goats. That's another name for brush goats or slick goats. They were brought here by the Spanish explorers to clear the land. They're good to kill Honey Locusts, and they run over thistles like bull dozers. They crush a thistle and eat it from the bottom up.

"Your goats'll be good as long as their teeth are good. Ten years, maybe. The only trouble is people's dogs kill goats and people get mad when you tell 'em about it.

"Another trouble is nannies. They go to nothin' after kidding. You can't tell what's the matter with 'em. There's somethin' they need. Don't let 'em kid after the 16th of March. It's too hot. Make wethers out of the billies so the nannies won't kid when it's hot. But when the nannies kid too early in the fall, they don't pick back up either. There's somethin' they need that they don't get. Mid-December to mid-February is the time for your nannies to kid. They'll do better.

"Goat meat is hard to sell. It makes people mad if they hear of you sellin' goats to eat. Eating goat meat makes people

16

mad. Call it Spanish Mutton or Roast Mutton or Boiled Mutton or Chili con Carne or Hot Dogs, then you can sell it. Then you can eat it.

"There's a man at the Harrison Stock Yard sells most of the goat meat around here. He gets orders for goats from Louisiana and Texas where they have a lot of goat meat barbecues.

"The big game preserves that have wild animals and exotic game animals will buy big wethers or billies with big horns. The kind of people who go to places like that shoot them for trophy animals. I guess they look like African animals or something — 'There's a big trophy goat — shoot it,' their guide tells them. If you have a big billy with big horns they'll pay $200 for it. They buy big mean hogs, too. The guides tell the hunters the goats and hogs are wild animals.

• • •

"Goats?" Brad Karnes asked. "All I know is goat-killing music rots the teenagers' minds. If there's a Hell, they're playing goat-killing music."

• • •

"I got cows," Ertie Youngblood said.

• • •

Iknew about everybody who spoke to me griped about goats in one way or another, but they weren't kidding me. They loved them. They couldn't live without them. As soon as I can get one of them good fence chargers from New Zealand, I'll put a hot wire around my place. I'll contact Jack Fancher for a Pyrenees dog, then go to the sale barn to buy me some brush goats. I'm ready to start goating.

CHAPTER 3

OZARK PROBLEMS AND FOLK REMEDIES

You're tired of messing with cattle marketeers who are thicker than cord wood and ruder than an automobile.

You're tired of the hog market hustlers thinking you're the sock that works down in the toe of their boot.

Your heart's hurtin' like it was drug on a dirt road.

Buyers look at you like constipated dogs.

Your head's the board fence the horses crashed through.

You're feeling as ineffective as a bent nail.

As confused as a new born calf.

As desperate as a leafless tree.

As defenseless as a turtle on a superhighway.

You sull up like an unpainted house, look in the mirror and see you're a mud ugly condemned to founder in sour silage for the rest of your natural life while your animals starve and your crops burn up.

You've had enough. From now on you're meaner'n barbed wire.

As serious as a ruptured appendix.

You got a thistle growing in your gut.

When you've cut your hay, you shake your fist at the clouds and shout, "Hell, let it rain! I don't care!"

When your chicken houses need walking, you say, "I don't care if it harelips the governor, I'm drinking coffee from can to cain't."

But one day, your calves are scoured-out, your goats are wormy; it's 10 below and the electricity's off — the heat lamps don't work and the sow's had a litter of pigs. You say, "I know the Lord don't need any more ignorant farmers. I'm finding me a life that ain't as futile as a bug climbing up the inside of a toilet."

But whoa! Don't go. You just need to turn your luck. Time to try some Ozark folk remedies. Pick up buckeyes. They're lucky. Collect live ladybugs in your fields and crickets in your house. They're lucky, too.

Brew sassafras and feverweed tea. It'll thin your blood, take your headaches away. Steep mullein leaves to heal your flaming sinus.

Bathe in fresh cow's milk. Feel it draw the poison from your body, mind, and soul. Feel it make you strong and take away your allergies, allowing you to face the most meaningful life there is, farming, again.

Peel some bark off of a white oak tree. Boil it in water to grow you some hair on top of your head and to improve your general health.

Drop alfalfa seed in your salad to bring the serenity needed to readjust to God's big acres. Then, before you take a walk around admiring your place, get some leaves off a pennyroyal. Rub them on your britches legs to keep the ticks and chiggers away.

Gather elderberry leaves. Mix them with mustard, turnip, or dandelion greens. Take bags of that to all your marketeers. Give lots of it to your buyers. They'll never be constipated again!

CHAPTER 4

CHARLEY MINICK

Charley's old home place is north of Berryville. You go on Highway 21 for ten miles. Pass the Cosmic Cavern and take the Hale cemetery road to the T. Turn left. Go less than a half mile. That's the place where Charley grew up on the right.

Before 1961, Charley raised chickens and hauled horses, mules, cows, feed, hay, and sawdust. Many days he'd scoop a load of sawdust onto his truck, take it to its destination, scoop it off, return to the sawmill, scoop on another load, take it to its destination and scoop it off. One day he said to himself, "Charley, this is too much scooping." In that moment he realized he was wearing out a truck and only getting by. When the truck wore out completely, he wouldn't have enough money to make a down payment on another one. Also, it hit him that he wasn't building up enough Social Security to live on when he retired from trucking.

The chickens he was raising weren't helping either. Every time a flock of chickens looked like they were going to make something, the feed bill went up.

Charley was getting full of days, as it says in the Bible, and he was worried. He knew he had to go somewhere to get a good job and work at it for fifteen or twenty years to make enough for a good retirement.

He decided on California, which at the time was booming.

His first job there was harvesting rice in Oroville in the Sacramento Valley.

The rice farmer Charley worked for prepared his ground as if he was going to plant wheat or oats, except the field had dikes around it. He submerged each field in two to eight inches of water and sowed the rice by airplane. In a few days, rice plants were growing on top of the water.

Many times, in order to harvest the grown rice with the old Caterpillar the farmer gave him to use, Charley had to bolt pieces of iron onto the tracks. He couldn't get any traction in the gumbo muck without them.

"In the dry weather the rice dust ate me up. I shook corn-starch and Johnson's talcum powder down my neck and buttoned my coveralls up tight to keep the dust out, but those measures didn't help. The dust still itched me. I was miserable."

Farming is like anything else, you have to be smart about it. Charley remembered one year after they had the oats, the wheat, and the rice harvested, another farmer wanted Charley to harvest his maize. Oh, he had a good crop of it. It was everywhere.

The farmer had bought a new combine which didn't have air conditioning like all the other farmers had. This el-cheap-o didn't even have a cab. This farmer drove the tractor in the sun and blistered while Charley ran the old tractor with a cab on it.

That farmer decided to run his in second gear, and he told Charley to run his in second gear, too. Charley ran it as the farmer said for about fifty yards before the machine clogged. He stopped to clean it out. This happened several times.

Charley said, 'I'm going to slow down.'

The farmer said, "No."

Both of them kept trying to harvest this field with their machines running like crazy. But the machines clogged up and they'd have to stop to clean them out.

"I got disgusted," Charley said. "I dropped my machine down into low gear without saying anything. When I was coming around where he was stopped to unplug his machine, I'd slip it up into second till I got around him. Then I dropped it down into low again. He never knew the difference.

"I'd learned back in the Ozarks that it pays a feller not to crowd things. This Californian never did learn that. When we finished that field, there were piles of maize all over it where he'd stopped to unclog his machine. What a waste."

When the summer and fall harvesting was over, Charley eased over to Mount Palomar, near the Imperial Valley.

One of the big reasons he moved to California was that when a job gave out in one place, he could move to another place. As many things as there were to do in California, he could work the year around.

In Mount Palomar, he worked on a turkey ranch with thousands of turkeys.

"That place like to worked me to death. There were actually three or four hours every day that I wasn't working at all. I had nothing to do but sleep. I'm not talking about in a regular eight-hour work day. I'm talking about in the whole day!

"I worked there long enough to see how it was. I didn't like it. It got so I didn't like the boss either. Somehow, I got one day off and slipped off down into Imperial Valley to a place called Brawley and got another job."

When he went back to the turkey ranch to give his quitting notice, the boss offered to raise his wages.

"No," Charley said, "that won't fix it."

Well, the boss wouldn't take that for an answer. He said he needed Charley.

Charley said, "I don't think I suit you exactly, and you don't suit me exactly either. I think I better move on."

He said, "You can do as you please."

So Charley did as he pleased. He headed for the Holly Sugar Mill in Brawley.

It was summer time. The temperature was 120 degrees in the shade, if there'd been any.

He crossed the desert at thirty-five miles per hour. That way his car didn't boil dry the way the other cars did.

In the sugar mill, he ran the belt that stored the sugar beets. He was working on a platform high enough up in the air that if there was any breeze at all, he'd get it. There was a roof over him—no sides.

The job was hard in a couple of ways. For one thing, he

was surrounded by workers who spoke Spanish. The owners worked immigrants—legal or illegal—whenever they could to save money. He couldn't talk to them the way he could talk to folks back in the Ozarks. Another thing was it was too hot.

He worked with one Mexican who turned out to be one of his best friends. Charley called him Blondie. He was a full blooded Mexican, and the blackest man he'd ever seen.

Blondie liked Charley. He offered to steal things from other folks to give to him, but Charley wouldn't let him.

"Blondie worked in the fields harvesting fruit and vegetables," Charley said. "I'd told him cantaloupe was my favorite melon, so when the crew he worked on finished harvesting them in a certain place, he'd tell me because they left many and I could go take a few home. They do the same thing with onions. In California, they don't pick fields clean."

At that sugar mill, he was responsible for two belts that dumped sugar beets in a v-shaped storage bin. He did all right. But because of the weather and working with strangers, he got blue. He was as blue as he could be.

Charley would stand there in that shed working those belts, sweating and thinking of Arkansas.

Remembering Arkansas

He thought of the time the music teacher came to that old Civil War cabin south of Oak Grove to tune the organ. He was real near sighted and a little bit short. He didn't come all the way up.

The reason he was tuning that organ was that he was stuck on the girl who lived there. She was one of his students. He was chewing tobacco and tuning away. He wasn't in any hurry about it. The girl's brothers were watching him. He was keeping his eye on their sister.

The organ was in the main part of the cabin. The kitchen-dining area was hooked on to the back of it. The music teacher didn't know that. He thought the main part was all there was to it.

He was still working away. He didn't have his mind on what he was doing. He was chewing tobacco and after awhile he had his lower lip stuck way out to keep from drowning.

Suddenly, the music teacher went over and opened what he thought was the back door and spit tobacco juice out into the middle of the kitchen!

The girl's brothers like to died they were so tickled. They had a real hoot and holler. They never let their sister forget it. That music teacher wasn't about to get her after that.

He thought about the time he and Ray, his trucking buddy, got a bunch of mules—six to be exact— and Mark Walker wanted four of them.

He had them tied with rope halters he'd plaited himself. He told Mark they were green mules not broke to lead. He said ok and gave them a check signed with a wavy line. They couldn't see a letter in his name. He and Ray took it to the bank immediately. They were worried, but they got the money with no problem.

They went back, put the mules in the truck loose in order

to get them all in, and hauled them to Mark's.

He directed them to back over to a certain spot to unload. He said they could lead the mules into the barn from there.

"What do you mean—lead them?" Charley asked him. "I told you these were green mules."

Mark threw a fit. He was a skinny fellow. Tall. Not big enough to do anything but threaten.

While he was going on, Charley climbed up on top of his truck.

"What are you doing?" Ray asked.

"I'm fixing to kick the mules out in the street. If you'll let the end gate loose..."

Ray reached for the end gate.

"No! Please don't do that!" Mark shouted. He knew those mules would be gone before their hooves hit the ground.

"Then cool it," Charley said, "this is nothing to blow up about."

"Well," he said, "back up to the chute. Unload them there."

"That's more like it," Charley said. He and Ray unloaded the mules just as slick as could be.

Mark started apologizing and kept it up till they left.

Charley and Ray laughed all the way back to Charley's place.

And he thought of T.J. Davis who ran the gas station at Oak Grove for years. T.J. was Tot Davis's son. Tot and Arnold Humbard's dad owned the tomato cannery that stood where Carolyn Kurbo's house is now.

Anytime Charley and Ray had more horses than they could carry, they used T.J.'s truck.

One time they went to Sand Springs, Oklahoma, to deliver fourteen horses and one mule. They came to Tulsa. T.J. was driving. He blew his horn at some car and the mule brayed. T.J. blew it again and the mule brayed again. So there they were, traveling through Tulsa—T.J. blowing his horn and the mule braying. The horn and the bray were about the same note, the same key. Charley and Ray almost laughed themselves sick.

Another time they were in Joplin. Charley was driving. He looked out the window and saw the shadow of one of the horses they were hauling. He was about half way out.

"We're losing one!" he yelled and pulled over to herd him in.

It was the old bob-eared horse—he'd had his ears froze off when he was a colt. Charley knew he was bad to jump when he bought him at the Berryville Sale Barn.

Charley remembered his friend T.J. Davis. Sometimes it was just he and T.J. by themselves hauling horses, and they talked a bunch.

"He was the best-hearted fellow I was ever around," Charley said. "T.J. told me about being wounded in Germany during WWII. They shot him in the arm and maybe through the body, I can't remember. He laid down by a log. When some of his buddies said they'd stay with him, he begged them to go on, leave him alone. He was so sore he said he'd rather die right then. He said he'd prayed through until he felt all right about dying. It was pitiful to hear him talk about it."

Another time Charley remembered was when he was hauling a bull to the sale barn for a neighbor and it jumped out of his truck there in Berryville. The bull rared up and climbed high enough on the side to roll over it. He hit the ground flat on his side. Stunned him. It may have broken a couple of ribs, Charley didn't know.

Before the bull came completely conscious, Charley took a twenty foot log chain and whipped it around his horns and chained him to the truck. Charley was scared to death the fall killed him. It relieved Charley when the bull stood up. He brought a good price at the sale, too.

Charley was hating Brawley worse every day. Remembering Arkansas helped him escape it in his mind while he was there. Oh, it was hot.

In the pits in California

One day he looked out and saw Ollie, his wife, and another woman driving up. Ollie said a call came in from the cannery in Oroville in northern California saying they wanted him to come up there and go to work.

He told her to call them back and tell them he'd be there.

"I finished out that day at Brawley, paid the rent, and we arrived in Oroville the next day. I'd started there in the rice and worked some part time in the peach cannery. I was glad to be back."

Charley worked on the peach pitting machine until he retired.

A person can't stay away from the Ozarks very long. All those years he and his wife were out in California, they kept coming back to visit the kids who were all married and away from home before they left. The kids came to visit them out in California, too.

Charley liked working in the peach cannery, but something bothered him. Even though they'd called him to come to work there, the superintendent—he was on his way out—wasn't going to put him on full time. The super knew Charley was a good hand, but he'd taken a dislike to him for some reason. He kept putting other workers in ahead of him. What he forgot and Charley didn't was the cannery was a union shop.

"After I'd been there a bit and saw how things were," Charley said, "I went into his office and told him if he didn't quit it I'd go to the union. I'd never done that way before, but I was fixing to.

"He fishtailed around for a minute and said they'd put this last fellow Adams ahead of me because they needed a plumber. When I heard that, I knew I had to call his bluff. Adams didn't know pipe threads from peach blight. He'd never plumbed one thing."

Bart, the fellow who was taking the superintendent's place, followed Charley out of the office. He'd heard the whole thing. He stopped him and said, "I'll have charge of this in a short time. I promise you one thing. When I take over, you're the next man to go on steady."

He followed up on his word. He not only put Charley on steady, he gave him top wage, which was five or six dollars an hour back then.

Some time after Charley signed on there, the man—Gene Johnson—in charge of repairing the peach pitting machines was about to quit. He told Charley he'd show him everything he knew. If Charley caught on, management would put him in the job.

"The other boys had wanted to know how to do Gene's job so they could get it. He wouldn't tell them. He'd laugh and tell Charley it had taken him years to learn what he knew. He wasn't going to let them in on it. He told Charley he'd do him a favor and tell him and he did.

One of the bosses, Harry, called Charley into his office to ask him if he thought he could handle Gene's job. Even though he never was much of a mechanic, Charley liked a good challenge. He'd been praying about it, so he told Harry, "I believe we can take care of it." Charley didn't tell him who "we" was.

"Talk about a challenge. Sometimes I'd tear a machine down that totally bewildered me. In the night I'd pray about it until something came to me. The next day I'd go and fix it. I have to give God credit for that."

Oh, does Charley remember Harry! Charley was on the peach pitter one morning (when he wasn't repairing them, he ran them). The other workers were at their places. Harry came out to tell them, "When you start up, throw every machine on wide open."

Harry didn't see they'd be starting production from a dead stop so they should start up easy. The way they always did.

Bosses can be so dumb. But you either run the machines the way the boss says or you don't run them.

The other workers muttered, "We can't do that. It won't work."

Charley said, "We'll run 'em that way till he hollers." They turned the machines on and peaches were moving through that cannery at top speed. Starting up fast that way put everything out of adjustment. But they kept going. They hadn't run thirty minutes before they had peaches spewed everywhere.

The workers left their machines to gather them up. They told Charley to do the same.

He said, "No, Harry said to run wide open."

They kept hollering for Charley to shut down. He didn't. Somebody went to get Harry.

Harry came back there. He looked at one big ol' tank. He saw the peaches running over the top of it, the peaches piled up knee deep around it.

Harry looked back at Charley just as pitiful, but Charley never let on he knew he was there.

He went over to Charley and said, "You're going to have to shut down."

"Harry, I could have told you we'd have to do that when you told us to start wide open."

They got that mess cleaned up. Harry began telling him how to get started again.

Charley told him, "No, Harry, let us take care of starting up and canning the peaches. You'll get all the peaches you want if you leave everything to us."

He said he would. He said he'd stay out of the way, and he did. Everything went fine after that.

Another time, the company'd bought a new tomato peeler. They'd switched from peaches to tomatoes by then. Bart had to figure out where to put it. It was a heavy awkward thing. Charley's crew had to set it up on I-beams so they could put metal pipes under it and roll it like a piece of furniture.

They set it down on the position Bart marked for it. They welded it to the I-beams and drilled holes beside it to screw it to the floor. They really planted it. It wouldn't move in an earthquake.

Next, they brought in the electricians to wire it and the plumbers to connect the pipes. They got it ready to run.

Three days later Bart came back there and said, "Guess what?"

"Where do you want it moved?" Charley answered.

"A little more than a foot forward," he said.

Charley didn't say anything. He and the others undid the pipes and wires. They unscrewed that machine from the floor. They jacked it up. They put pipes under it and rolled it forward about fourteen inches and anchored it down.

Later, Harry marked the flume (that's the trough that carries the tomatoes and water from the tomato peeler) and they attached it. Bart came by again. He saw the flume.

"Who done that?" he asked.

"We did," Charley answered.

"Harry told you to do it, didn't he?"

Charley nodded as Harry came back.

"Harry, how in the world do you expect this thing to work?" Bart shouted. "You've got this end higher than that end. How's the water supposed to get away? It can't. Water don't flow up hill!"

Charley wondered how Harry kept his job.

The events in this story are only a few of the memories Charley has of California. He's glad he went. He gets a better retirement as a result of working there. He's also glad to be back here in Carroll County. "There's no place in this world like the Ozarks!"

Charley's dog tales

One time George traded a dog to Willy. Willy was proud until the dog turned out to be a sheep-killing dog. Willy went to see George and said, "I'd rather have that dog as any dog I've ever owned, but I'd like to know why you didn't tell me it was a sheep-killing dog."

"Well," George answered, "The guy I got it from didn't tell me. I thought he wanted it kept a secret."

Another time, George traded another dog for an ol' long, country looking hound.

Willy came by and asked, "George, is she any good?"

George said, "Yeah, she treed three or four possums last night."

"What kind of mouth she got? Is she one of those short mouths that chops her bark or a long mouth?" Willy asked.

"Oh," George said, "she's a long mouth. Sometimes she barks so long she has to back up to get it all out."

George lived in Grandview, and one day he was fixing to go to California. He'd raised a pair of good running fox dogs. They run awful good.

Willy'd heard people talk of George's dogs and he wanted them.

When he went to see George to try to trade, George told him the dogs were full brothers. He said, "One of them is a curly tail. His tail curls plumb over to make a complete turn. When he runs, his tail curls. It always curls."

Willy said, "I've never heard of that. How much curl is there? Does it curl down tight?"

George answered, "Why yes, it curls down so tight he can't reach the ground with his hind feet."

CHAPTER 5

BLACK MOLLY'S BABY

As an Arkansas farmer who has to work in town to support himself, I'm never sure what I'll discover when I get home: I might find the hogs in the feed room, the horses in the garden, or the goats on the neighbor's roof.

When I counted the cows one afternoon and discovered that little Black Molly was missing, I figured it was one of those times. I searched for at least twenty minutes before I spotted her standing quietly by an uprooted tree in the fringe area between the sloping pasture and the gulch. I spotted the impossible, too.

When I had brought her home from the sale barn the previous summer, I thought that Black Molly was too young and too small to be bred anytime soon, so I hadn't been watching her. But satyric Curly, my five-year-old Hereford bull, evidently had a different opinion. He must've lured her out into the bosky hills some months before and bred her while I wasn't looking, because there she was now, with about a yard of membrane and two hooves, ivory white and tawny brown, protruding from her birth canal.

Since I believed she'd never bear that calf by herself, I knew I had to help. As I crept toward her, I mooed softly to assure her I could be trusted. She didn't buy this, and trotted off into the setting sun. With a cold March wind cutting through my barn jacket, I followed her, hoping she'd calm down and let me pull that calf. But she kept moving toward the wilderness that bordered the pasture. Running as fast as I could across the uneven ground, I circled to head her off. If she tramped into that forty acres of jungle, the only things to find her would be the coyotes.

I turned her just before she could crash into the woods, and she fled back to the uprooted black oak. As I approached, I masqueraded as a cow again, but she shied away, and I backed off.

Realizing I'd better get serious and remove that calf quickly, I hurried to the barn, picked up a rope and a pan of feed, grabbed a pair of cotton gloves that had most of the fingers worn through, and rushed back to Black Molly. She was gone.

I listened. The rustling leaves and cracking limbs told me she was moving west along the ridge toward the frontier forty that I'd just herded her away from. With tree limbs grabbing at my red stocking cap, I crunched after her across the rocky ridge, dodging grapevines and spicy cedars while carrying the feed pan and rope. A black form on the ground startled me, and I thought for a moment that Black Molly had fallen and died, but it was only a charred stump from an ancient fire. I pressed on until I found her near a dense thicket. Fortunately, she hadn't entered the woods.

She watched warily while I placed the feed near her and stepped back to block the opening to her little nook. Eventually she began to eat, and I tried to lasso her. A branch deflected my throw, and the rope wormed limply across her shoulders as she peeled out, knocking me down and throwing flint rock and dried leaves three feet into the air.

By the time I clambered to my feet, Black Molly was back at the uprooted oak, no doubt thinking she was rid of me. But I coiled the rope, retrieved the feed pan, and strode after her. I got about five yards before I tripped and fell, jamming two of the fingers on my right hand. Confident that the pain would redeem my sins for at least six months, I let it burn through me before sitting up to find that, miraculously, most of the feed was still in the pan.

The pain finally became tolerable, plus—yee, haw!—Black Molly had moved to join the rest of the herd grazing in the open pasture. Left-handed, I snatched the lasso and feed pan and walked toward her carefully, squinting in the lowering sunlight. I put the pan down close to her and encircled it with the loop of the rope. With the other end in my hand, I stepped off to the side a couple of yards to wait. She evidently wasn't worried about me, maybe because lots of her friends were nearby. She poked her nose into the feed immediately after I moved out of the way and began to eat heartily. I yanked on the rope and pulled the noose securely around her neck.

Startled, Black Molly pulled backward trying to free herself. The rope tightened, but I was able to hold on because she's so small. I began moving her down the slope toward the uprooted tree by alternately pulling the rope and taking up slack until I could tie her to a root on about a dozen feet of line. It should have been shorter, but she went spraddle-legged. She wasn't giving another inch.

I went behind Black Molly and grabbed the slick hooves of the calf. They slipped from my gloved hands once or twice before I was able to grip them securely enough to begin pulling and tugging with all my might. The effort wasn't affecting anything until her abdominal walls began to expand and contract. Almost immediately, a nose appeared in a gush of liquid and a mess of membrane. I had barely swabbed the film from the calf's nostrils (so it could breathe if it was alive) when it slid back, and the nose disappeared.

Hoping my hundred and eighty pounds would disengage it, I clutched the legs and tried to sit down without giving any slack. It didn't work. Briefly, I yearned for the twenty pounds I had lost by giving up ice cream and pie every night. My hands slipped from the wet hooves and I staggered backward as Black Molly bolted.

The rope swung her around, and she climbed over the embankment made by the uprooted tree and into the depression behind it. I followed her up, lost my footing in the crumbling dirt, and—naturally—used my jammed fingers to break my fall. White-hot tines of pain raced up my arm. Grimacing, I raised my face to the sky and worried about catching the undulant fever. I pulled off my gloves, wet with blood and slime.

Despite the pain in my hand, I got up and slogged over that mound to grab the hooves and pull and tug some more. Black Molly was so narrow through the hips that nature would never push that calf out for her. I didn't know if I had any time left; if the umbilical cord had broken, the calf either had smothered or would do so shortly.

I tugged harder. I thought I was strong, but I was making no progress with this problem whatsoever. My muscles were hardly functioning. They felt dead, yet they hurt. I released the hooves for a moment and opened and closed my wooden fists, trying to revive them.

I grabbed the hooves again, and just as I began to yank on them, Black Molly's body contracted so severely her stomach caved in, and she fell down. There she was, an under-sized cow with a dangerously large Hereford calf inside her trying to get out while she was lying on her side with a tether choking her.

I thought of going for my neighbor. I thought of going for the vet. Instead, I put all the strength I had into removing that calf. It moved as though it were buried in mud. It came out a bit as I pulled, but slid back as soon as I stopped. Bewildered, I paused. I didn't know what to do, but Black Molly's rasping breath inspired me to try again. I was straining on those hooves when another deep spasm surged through her body. I felt the calf clear something.

With arms barely responding and shoulders aching, but with hope still alive, I tugged weakly on the calf. My efforts accomplished nothing until another spasm hit Black Molly. I felt the calf move.

Gasping, I tugged and tugged. The calf oozed forward... there was its head... then a little more... there were its shoulders... then came its belly —come on, a little farther! — there were its hips...there! It emerged, flopped to the ground, and lay there as motionless as a pile of wet burlap sacks.

I tore the membrane from its body, hoping it wasn't dead, and wiped out its nose again. It wasn't breathing. Urgently, I pressed down on its rib cage. Push...let up. Push...let up. Don't push down so hard, I told myself. Don't break its ribs. Then when I pushed and let up again, it kicked and rolled a little bit. It was alive.

I walked in front of Black Molly, who still lay on her side, wheezing. I tried to undo the lasso from around her neck, but the rope was pulled too tight. I stepped over the root and untied the rope, marveling that it had held. Now I undid the lasso and slipped it over her head as she raised up. Thinking that it was all over and I would see a mother-calf reunion, I stepped back to watch, but Black Molly lunged to her feet and sprinted off into the twilight.

I stared after her helplessly. Had she rejected her calf? The chances of it living without some of her milk were weak, although the calf didn't seem worried; it lay curled up among the rocks, as quiet as still water.

I took the feed pan, jiggled it loudly, and called to Black Molly. I mooed a couple of times, too. Macho Curly, hoping I was a new concubine, I guess, approached, but stopped at a distance to sniff and stare.

As I leaned over to put down the feed pan, I noticed the calf was shivering, and I realized I was cold. Small wonder; my jacket and gloves and jeans were slimy and my hands and wrists were wet with afterbirth. Furthermore, my nose was running.

Maybe if I left, nature would bring Black Molly back. I started walking to the house. As I did, I saw a form in the deepening dusk moving toward the calf, mooing anxiously. I stopped to watch and saw the stubby form edge in closer to the calf. It was Black Molly. What more could I do but stay in the house for a while, hoping she'd stay with her calf until

it suckled out some colostrum?

Once inside, I dropped my soiled clothing into the washer and took a shower. The hot water soothed my swollen fingers and my aching shoulders; a meal of reheated beef stew renewed my energy.

Certainly enough time had passed to allow Black Molly to tend to her calf. Using a flashlight, I returned to the fallen

oak. Its roots loomed like a Medusa. I looked around fruit-
lessly. Inasmuch as the entire herd was still grazing on the
hillside, Black Molly shouldn't be far away. But where? I
couldn't help but wonder if she had allowed her calf to nurse,
and if it was still alive.

I flashed around in the trees and out on the hillside until I
came upon her in the fescue, licking her calf vigorously. For
the first time I noticed that its body was as black as hers, and
it had a white face, like Curly. It was half as big as she was,
and God, it looked swell.

Black Molly mooed nervously and moved so that she was
broadside between the calf and me. I dodged around her and
knelt beside it. When I lifted its leg, I saw a soft little sack of
testicles; it was a bull. Tomorrow, I would put a rubber band
around that little pouch and turn him into a steer. I released
his leg and looked into his face. He had a black patch around
one eye. This hefty fellow may have been with Long John
Silver on Treasure Island. I'll just name him Jolly Roger.

I stepped back, and Jolly Roger shifted his weight awk-
wardly, stood up, and went to his mother's bag to nurse. Tears
came to my eyes, and I headed for the house.

CHAPTER 6

PREGNANT BRIDGE

Going south out of Berryville on County Road 35, you'll come to where the Osage River runs around the foot of Pension Mountain. A new bridge crosses the river just upstream from Simmons Ford, where the old cement slab called Pregnant Bridge used to be. People called it Pregnant Bridge — not because of the young people who parked out there, as many think — but because in the '40's when Dotson and Smith built it, they didn't set the piers on solid rock. The long, skinny thing sagged as soon as they lifted the forms, leaving a hump in the middle. That's how it got its name, from that bellied-out hump.

Not far from that part of the Osage River lay the Patty farm, home of Eartle and Edith Patty and their children. Eartle remembers some harrowing times at Simmons Ford before they built Pregnant Bridge,

Eartle Patty

I didn't care what they called that bridge, I was proud somebody built it. I could begin sleeping nights.

Before Pregnant Bridge, folks who lived on and around Pension Mountain had to brave the Osage going to and from Berryville with horses and wagons. When the river was low, their teams pulled the wagons through it slick as a whistle. During the wet parts of the year, when the Osage swelled up as deep as six, eight, ten feet, or more, lots of folks got stuck. Then they'd come after me. I'd get up, dress, hitch up my broncs, and go pull them out. On winter nights, sometimes it was blue cold. Ice'd hang from my horses' legs.

There were neighbors with teams who lived closer to the ford than I did. They was willing enough neighbors, they'd take their horses down there and hook them to a stuck wagon, and their horses let on as if they was pulling, yet they wasn't turning a wheel. They was faking. They'd lean and strain as though they was killing themselves when they wouldn't of pulled ten pounds if they'd been hitched to it. Their teams was smart. They didn't want to get a reputation for pulling.

I remember one night after I'd gone to bed, Claude Cisco woke me up. He lived farther up Pension Mountain than we did. He and his son had gone to Berryville to get a load of feed.

He crossed the ford all right going. Coming back, he discovered the Osage was swirling fast and deep. During the day, rain had fallen somewhere up the valley; the May rise had started.

His horses didn't want any part of that river, but Claude forced them to pull his wagon as far as the middle, where they balked for good.

He climbed down into the river to unhook them. The first horse he unhooked was the first one that balked, and it was swept down- stream. Claude had to swim to rescue it. Was he mad!

He tied the other horse to a sycamore, got his son, and they rode the first horse back to Doff Ross's place to trade for a horse that'd pull. The sun had set a long time ago, but in those days, swapping horses was like swapping knives. A man could do it anytime.

But even with a different horse, Claude was nervous about hitching his team to a wagon sitting out in the river with water rushing over it. He left both horses tied to the tree, crossed the river, and walked about a mile to get me and Prince and Ol' Coley — my broncs. Their reputation for pulling had spread all over Pension Mountain.

I rolled out of bed and harnessed them to the wagon and headed for Simmons Ford. A man couldn't ask for better horses than them broncs. They were horses that'd pull. They didn't fake it.

Fifty years ago, broncs was shipped into northwestern Arkansas in bunches of fifty or sixty from Colorado, Montana, and Wyoming, several times a year. A man could go to a stockyard, as in Harrison, say, and match himself up a team.

When we arrived at the ford, my broncs didn't hesitate; they waded in, which pleased me because I aimed to hook my wagon to Claude's, pull it out, and crawl back in bed. I had some haying to do the next day.

I noticed the moonlight shining on the water rushing over his wagon. It looked pretty to me, but as Prince and ol' Coley splashed closer, they must've thought his wagon was a monster, I reckon, 'cause they bolted past it and didn't stop till they was on the other side. I turned them around and tried again. They bolted past it again. I don't know how many times that happened. I couldn't hold them.

I told Claude — he and his son were in the back of my wagon — "Put your son up here with me. We'll try this another way. Hook one end of this log chain to the rear of this wagon. When my broncs charge past your wagon, dive in and hook this other end to the axle. Don't get hung up in the chain. I can't hold these broncs."

I drove into the river. As Prince and ol' Coley commenced stampeding past his wagon, Claude dove in, fastened the chain around his rear axle, and yanked his arms back in the nick of time, 'cause —boy howdy! —when those broncs took up the slack, they was gone! They pulled his wagon out with

no trouble, except we were on the wrong side of the river.

We hitched Claude's horses to his wagon and loaded the wet feed into my wagon. Thinking he'd be safer with me, Claude told his boy to climb on top of the wet burlap sacks.

Then he drove his team, pulling an empty wagon, across the river—his horses floundering all the way.

After he made it, I guided Prince and ol' Coley upstream until we were about halfway across, where I meant to turn them downstream and let the current carry most of the weight of the wet feed into shallow water. What I didn't know was that the current had washed out a big hole exactly where I was turning. My broncs all but disappeared in it. Whooee! I looked for them and saw only their ears sticking up.

"Hold onto my boy, Eartle! Don't let him drown! Oh, my boy's a goner!" Claude cried, seeing his son with water up to his chin.

"Hold it, Claude. He ain't drowned yet. My broncs'll pull us out of here in a minute." If everything hangs together, I added to myself. I was afraid the power of the Osage surging against my wagon would break something. If it did, Prince and ol' Coley would run off, leaving me and Claude's boy to fend for ourselves.

Fortunately, the wagon held together. The broncs pulled us to safety. Me and Claude loaded the feed onto his wagon.

"Thanks for pulling me out, Eartle. I'll help you if I catch you in a tight some time," Claude said, adding, "I'd give anything to have a team like yours — a team that pulls!"

As I followed Claude in my wagon toward home — I was tired— I wondered if he would give anything for Prince and ol' Coley if he knew as much about them as I did. They were dangerous.

To harness ol' Coley, you had to be careful to come up to

him slowly, from the front. To harness Prince, you first had to stand and talk to him. If you didn't he'd rear up and paw you.

I told my brother Fay of Prince's way, but one day when he was helping me, he forgot and reached around him to fasten his breastplate without speaking to him. I saw Prince rear up to paw him. I grabbed for the check lines and missed.

Luckily, ol' Coley threw his head up just then and Prince's leg came down across the top of ol' Coley's neck, allowing only the cork of Prince's shoe to glance across Fay's head, gashing it and knocking him flat. If ol' Coley hadn't thrown his head up when he did, Prince would've killed Brother deader than a hammer. Prince was mean that way.

On another day, Edith, the kids, Fay, and me was going to Berryville. Fay was in the front of the wagon with me. I had the reins. Edith and the kids was sitting on a board across the back of the wagon.

Everything was fine until Prince and ol' Coley got hot.

Fay wanted to stop at the creek and water them. That's the way he was, always petting animals and giving in to them. I wasn't that way.

Anyway, Fay kept on about it, so I stopped.

The WPA'd been blasting there — remember, this was in the '30's. Rocks was scattered everywheres, some of them bigger than armchairs. As Fay climbed down to loosen the reins to let the broncs drink, a black calf jumped the fence off to one side of us, scaring them. Prince sprang back and ol' Coley jumped sideways, snapping the wagon tongue in two. Those broncs ran, dragging the wagon across the river and over the rocks.

Edith and the kids was thrown from their seat to the bed of the wagon. The kids was just a-jumping and a-squalling back there. You could of heard them a couple of miles away.

I braced my feet and pulled back to stop the broncs. Instead, they yanked me off that wagon seat. I fell beside the front wheel, holding on to the reins like a dog. Fay was hanging on to Prince's hame strap, trying to stop him. I was dragging across the ground. Neither of us could let go — Edith and the kids was still in the wagon.

The wagon wheel — it had a strip of iron around the rim, iron-tired, we called them — rolled over my arm, taking the left rein away. I grabbed the right rein with both hands. Naturally, the broncs veered off to the right, with one of them galloping around the north side of a boulder and the other galloping around the south side.

My wagon crashed against that boulder and stopped those broncs cold, so I jumped up to help Edith and the kids.

By the time I got to them, the kids was climbing out of the wagon, sniffling. Edith, her legs beat black and blue, was calming them. Donald, our youngest boy, looked up at the wagon and said, "Them broncs tore us's wagon all to hell!" Edith and I had heard the word before, but not from any of our kids. We had to laugh at the way he said it.

Realizing we'd passed Leo Bunch's place a little ways back, we decided to return to ask him if we could borrow his wagon. Fay jumped on ol' Coley and that bronc leaped clear to the middle of the creek. They went across a-bucking and a-snorting — I followed on foot.

"I saw you go by," Leo said. "What happened to your wagon?"

I told him about the calf jumping the fence and causing the broncs to smash the wagon.

"Yep, you can borrow mine," Leo said. "It's setting by the barn."

We hitched both broncs to his wagon and went to town. I was foolish then, putting my family in a wagon behind broncs like Prince and ol' Coley. I wouldn't do it today for nothing. Back then, I was young. When I got hold of a mean horse, I couldn't wait to hitch him up to show him who was boss.

Another time, Prince and ol' Coley like to killed me and Edward, our oldest son. I'd bought a new harness, and we'd taken the broncs up on Pension Mountain to plow a patch of ground to plant tomatoes, 'cause the higher tomatoes grow, the better they taste.

We were about done when a storm came up out of the east. The wind was blowing; lightning was flashing; thunder was booming; and rain was falling in sheets. Hurrying, Edward and I unhitched the broncs from the plow to hook them to the wagon.

I hollered at him, "Son, be sure to fasten the lines short enough to the neck yoke they can't pull it off the end of the tongue!"

He tried, but, being young and in a hurry, he never did it the way I said. We weren't a hundred and fifty yards down that mountain when the neck yoke came off, dropping the tongue, of course, which commenced swinging, whopping Prince on his legs and then whopping ol' Coley on his. The broncs took off down that road like lightning was striking their butts. Again, I couldn't hold them.

At the first curve, they left the road and went off into the woods. I shouted to Edward, "Get down, son! Get down! Crawl under the seat, go to the back of the wagon. Grab the end gate and swing yourself out, but don't let go. Run behind the wagon till you get your balance, then turn loose. Once you're out, I'll jump. Let these wild broncs have this wagon!"

Edward disappeared under the seat. I thought he was doing what I said until I looked back and saw the little feller sitting against the end gate, wet as a wash rag.

Desperately, I yelled, "Get out, Edward. Get out son, before these broncs turn this wagon over and kill us both!"

Turning to the front, I saw the broncs were hightailing it toward two trees too close together for the wagon to pass between. I yanked on the reins, but they paid me no mind.

The front right wheel rolled up the tree, tipping the wagon up so that I was thrown backwards instead of forward. I heard the doubletree snap and saw Prince and ol' Coley get thrown together in such a way they butted heads. Was they mad! They reared up and pawed those trees until all the bark was off.

The rain was still pouring down. Oh, wet! We were like drowned rats. I don't know why I grabbed Edward and ran—nothing was going anywheres. I carried him away from there and checked him good. He wasn't hurt like I was. I was black and blue all over and madder than hell. I was wanting to kill both of them broncs; they'd torn my new harness all to pieces.

That wasn't the last thing they done, either.

Every Saturday morning, Edith and me and the kids went to town. Knowing my broncs didn't take long to get to Berryville, neighbors would come to my place to catch a ride. I'd been telling them I was afraid Prince and ol' Coley would hurt somebody some day, but folks were sideboard to sideboard in our wagon anyways. I didn't care for them going. I was just afraid of what might happen.

One Saturday, we were coming back from town with a wagon full of feed, groceries, and neighbors, when Prince and ol' Coley overtook another neighbor. He had a team of mules so slow you had to set stakes to see if they was moving. My broncs wanted to go around him, but I hate to pass a neighbor; I held them back.

Edith said to let the broncs go or they'd get tangled up and run away with us. I loosened the reins and—boy howdy!— my broncs was gone.

We'd scarcely passed the mules when a rear wheel came off my wagon and rolled up past Prince and ol'Coley, spooking them. They snorted, jumped, and away we went, with the axle dragging on the ground and the wagon pitching sideways.

At the next sharp curve, I turned them up on the bank into the fence, stopping them. I looked back to see if everybody was all right, and saw the neighbors going over my end gate one after the other like sheep a-jumping a fence. Everybody, including Edith and the kids, went home afoot that day. The neighbor with the old mules stopped to help me put on the wagon wheel.

The next Saturday morning, Edith and the kids said they wasn't going to town. None of the neighbors came over, either. I went to Berryville by myself and came back from Berryville by myself that Saturday. I can't remember any neighbors riding to town with me after that. They learned I wasn't just talk: broncs are dangerous.

Twelve or thirteen years later, I was plowing a field. A farmer stopped and asked, "Eartle, how much will you take for that black? He's a perfect match for one I've got."

I was using a tractor mostly by then and I was tired of working with Prince and ol' Coley, so I let ol' Coley go for fifty dollars. I took Prince to the Harrison sale barn the next sale they had. I told them how to handle him. I heard later that one of the hands threw a rope on Prince without having a talk and he reared up and pawed him—like to killed him. Prince was mean that way. Prince and ol' Coley are gone now, but I'm glad I owned that pair of wild broncs. They were horses that weren't afraid to pull.

CHAPTER 7

BUTTERCUP

There was this cow — I bought her as a heifer at the Green Forest Sale Barn. I intended to buy her low, but somebody ran me up. She cost me a bunch of good money.

Her eyes looked moody, so on the way home I named her Buttercup, hoping to improve her disposition.

I gave her the shots and put rubber bands on her horns. The right one fell off but the left one didn't. As it came further out of her head it curved down instead of up, and she somehow got her left ear scrunched in between it and the side of her head. She must have thought it looked cute because, even though I flipped it out whenever I could, by the next morning, she always had it stuck back in there.

Plus she ate some Fescue Fungus and her tail went bald. I gave her the medication. Two hairs grew back.

Then she got bred. Cows gestate in 283 days — 9 months, 13 days —but I didn't know when Buttercup'd calve because Deuteronomy, the bull, ashamed to let the world know he'd mate with anything that moos, led her to the far forty and bred her in the dark.

It was perfect timing, though. Early the next February (temperature 32 degrees) found her in the muck in the one low place on my farm where a couple of spindly oaks, a few sprouts, one or two scrub cedars, and a thick patch of briars clump together.

This low place was always a quagmire of coagulated mud. Buttercup was up to her ankles in it, chewing her cud contentedly. There was a puddle with a paper thin coating of broken ice behind her. Her calf was lying in it.

Fear shot through me. Buttercup dropped her calf in a frozen mud puddle? Was she crazy?

Carrying the wet, sticky, shivering thing to the barn to lay it down on dry bedding, I noticed it was too limp; its eyes weren't focused; and clots of stringy mucous dripped from its nose.

Buttercup hadn't followed me. With grunge all over my gloves, my barn coat, my jeans, I went back to the low place to bait her in with range cubes and found her gulping down her afterbirth. As the bloody sheaths of dark red and gristle white tissue, with bulbous sacs of murky liquid hanging from  them, disappeared, my stomach lurched.

Inside the barn, with the door shut to keep out the biting wind, the calf wasn't breathing. I straddled it to push gently on its ribs. It choked. It coughed. The mucous running from its nose became bloody, but it started breathing.

I drove Buttercup closer. She looked at her calf absently. She smelled it and walked away to pull some hay from a bale stacked beside the aisle

I carried the calf to her and tried to stand it on its wobbly feet to nurse. The calf sagged like a loose sack of sugar. I tried to hold it up, but my arms began aching so badly, I let it go. I tried raising its head to connect with a nipple. Buttercup kicked it away.

Angrily, I drove her to the head squeeze, milked out a quart or so of colostrum, and poured it in a bottle. Going to the calf, I pushed the black rubber nipple into its mouth.

It wasn't interested. I squeezed the bottle. The calf wouldn't swallow. Milk ran down the outside of its throat. But it was still breathing. Weakly, it tried to suck the nipple. I squeezed the bottle, shooting a stream of milk down its throat. The calf choked, coughed.

"Don't drown it, Stupid," I told myself. "You're supposed to be bringing this thing to life."

Its jaws moved again, feebly. As soon as my heart jumped with hope, it quit. Its head dropped to the floor. I drove Buttercup closer to enlist her help. She showed no interest. "You want me to run that TV ad by you, Buttercup? It says, 'Life is a wonderful choice!' Choose it! Let's go!"

Then I heard the calf sigh gently. Its life was over.

Buttercup looked at me, her eyes...her eyes...all of a sudden I wondered if she dropped this calf in the freezing water deliberately. What did she know about raising a calf that I didn't? Didn't she like having a calf nursing and butting her bag for milk?

What plans did this crumple-horned, one-eared, bald-tailed, reluctant-mother have for her free time? Was she wanting to go to the moon with the cow that jumped over it? Was she wanting the fun and frolic of the far forty without accepting any of the responsibility? Did she want to get on a safe sex program? Did she want her tubes tied?

I could wonder all day. She'd never tell. My only course of action was to put her back with Deuteronomy and wait for nine months and thirteen days to see if she was an expensive free loader or if this was all an accident.

CHAPTER 8

THE HOG AND THE HONEY LOCUST

The Professor of Cow Ponds called me yesterday from the Ford Mountain airport. He'd flown in on his way to Central Arkansas to attend a meeting about the removal of green scum from farm ponds. He called them "agricultural impoundments."

"Big Brother, my plane's made an emergency landing for repairs. Come out and tell me about yourself!" he said.

When I arrived at the airport, a mechanic was using a ball peen hammer to fine tune the airplane engine for take-off. The Professor of Cow Ponds and I sat outside on the shady side of the pilot's lounge. Dust devils swirled across the runway as I mentioned to the Professor how the pounding noise from the mechanic's hammer triggered memories of brush hogging the Ford Mountain farm he and I'd grown up on.

"Yes," I said, meaning to get a say in before he got started, "I brush hog the hilly farm each year trying to control the horse nettle, thistles, sassafras sprouts. I'm afraid my Ford tractor will turn over on one of the steep pastures and crush me..."

"Let me tell you about fear," he interrupted. "You don't know fear if you haven't tangled with a razorback hog! You talk about fear...It happened after Doug and I'd been hunting quail over on Little Indian Creek. I was carrying the .20

gauge shotgun you gave me. It had #8 bird shot in it—I still have that gun. It works good. Part of the stock is broken away. The crack that led to that is from this very story I'm about to tell you.

"I was coming across Philpot's Bottom toward Barley's Ridge without any birds. We hadn't had a bit of luck. Doug had already gone home.

"Suddenly, I saw a boar in the middle of a clearing. He was rooting along getting acorns. He didn't know I was there. I stopped in my tracks to admire his humongous tusks. I wasn't afraid. You remember, I'd been around hogs before.

"Saying to myself this must be one of those Razorback hogs, I visualized peppering it with bird shot. With great glee I imagined it leaping about and squealing.

"With absolutely no thought that this hog could be dangerous, I up and blasted away. I hit it dead center. Like lightning, it wheeled around and charged with its satanic eyes set on me .

"The sound of thundering hog's hooves pounding the earth toward me drove the glee from me. I imagined his yard-long tusks piercing my backside. I knew exactly what King David meant in the Bible when he said, 'I am poured out like water.'

"I had little strength yet I was able to hurl myself at a nearby tree to climb to safety, but I didn't find safety, I found sharp thorns. I felt them sticking into my hands and arms. I cried out in pain. Of all things—I'd hurled myself at a honey locust!

"I was sweating. I knew I'd gone way too far this time.

Judgement Day was at hand. Behind me was a maddened boar ready to rip me to shreds. In front of me was a honey locust ready to impale me on its thorns. Talk about the rock

and the hard place—what was I to do?

"An oak sapling about four inches thick a few feet from that honey locust answered my question. Zing! Like a monkey I went up that tree as far as I could. Looking down, I saw the razorback rubbing its tusks against the trunk.

"'Oh, dear God, it's cutting the tree down. It'll get me for sure. Where's my gun?

"I'd dropped it! It's lying beside the tree!

"Now, the grunting, slobbering hog was jumping up to grab my leg in its mouth and haul me down. Its snout wasn't far below my foot. I sweated. My gun was on the ground beside the tree—that's how the stock got cracked. That razorback landed on it when it came down from jumping for my feet.

"I wished for that gun with all my heart. I wanted to stick it in its mouth, pull the trigger, and bring this adventure to an end. But I didn't have the gun. The hog had it.

"My hands ached from holding myself up out of its reach. After awhile, it quit jumping after me and moved away to an area where the trees were thicker. It returned once to look up at me and snort ferociously. Then it jogged back into the thicket. It wasn't fooling me. It planned to wait in there until I fell out of the tree so it could come out and get me.

"Darkness began to thicken, compounding my terror and nullifying the hope I'd placed in my prayers that said I'd never pepper a hog with bird shot again if I could have another chance"

"Still gripping the young oak tree tightly, the pain in my hands became unbearable. Loosening my grip on the tree, I slid soundlessly to the ground. The wind rustling in the leaves made me think that boar was lurking in the shadows, ready to chomp a bite out of my thigh.

"Cautiously, I walked out a ways from the tree and waited.

If I heard his hooves booming toward me from the thicket, I was ready to zing back up that tree. I heard only what was probably chipmunks or rabbits or wind. I waited a few more minutes. No devil hog jumped out at me.

Suddenly, without a plan, I took out across Philpot's Bottom and got on the road for home. You won't believe this, but when I got there, my hands were empty. I forgot to pick up my gun.

"The next day I was scared to go back. I figured that hog would be there waiting for me. I wondered if it picked up the gun and took it to its den during the night.

"As afraid as I was, I sneaked into the thicket that next afternoon and found the gun. The fear I'd felt for that hog was pure, but it had gone away. I swaggered out of there like John Wayne."

The Professor of Cow Ponds was grinning. He'd told a good story and he knew it. But the first say doesn't matter that much. It's the last say people remember. So I said to the cow pond expert, "That's nothing, Little Brother. One time I was brush hogging the steep side of a pasture over on..."

"RRRRROMMMMMMM-BBBBRRRUUUMMM. GGGGGRRRRNNN-WHMMM!" The plane motor roared to life. The Professor motioned through a cloud of blue smoke for me to help him get aboard. I picked up his three brief-cases and hurried along beside him.

"Little Brother!" I shouted, trying to get the last say over the racket of the backfiring engines, "It was while you were at the university learning about cow ponds. I was brush hogging the pasture that practically rises straight out of the west hollow. You talk about fear..."

The Professor grabbed the briefcases I was carrying, "Thanks, Big Brother," he said. "After the meeting, I'll be examining agricultural impoundments in Central Arkansas for several weeks. Then it's back to Nebraska for me. 'Bye."

He disappeared into his plane. I stood there with my mouth open, watching the landing wheels slap the treetops as the plane struggled like a goony bird for altitude.

CHAPTER 9

THIS LITTLE PIGGY

Rickey, his wife, and their five children were living on his in-law's farm. He was attending the university, hoping to get a job that would allow him to get out on his own.

He knew what his in-laws were saying about the Chester White sow a farmer over in Metalton offered him: "Stay away from raising hogs. You don't have time. You don't have the background. We raise cows here, not hogs. Hogs are dangerous."

He took Big Pinky, anyway. Any baby pigs she had would be worth good money.

Rickey strung up a couple of wires to make a pen with a spring-fed branch in it. He plugged in an electric charger, set up a self-feeder, and introduced Big Pinky to Little Blacky, a boar he bought. Three months, three weeks, and three days later Big Pinky had 12 piggies: eight boars and four gilts.

Rickey knew he should cut back the tusks and tails of all the piggies and castrate the boars as soon as possible. The sale barn paid less for piggies with uncut tails and tusks and less for boars that weren't castrated. Also, he'd heard that piggies not only get stronger by the minute, they get faster, and their mamas get more possessive. Woe to the unsuspecting hog farmer who gets between a mama sow and her piggies.

But what with helping his wife Jeanne raise the children,

helping his father-in-law with the cattle, and doing the home-
work for his university courses, it was a blazing afternoon in
July, a month later, before he stole the time to work the piggies.

Sterilizing his pocket knife and finding his tusk and tail
clippers, he enlisted his six-year-old nephew Alan—his own
sons were still in diapers—to help him bow a sixteen-foot
hog panel into the bed of his old yellow Chevy pickup. He
didn't have a stock rack.

Rickey figured he would step into Big Pinky's pen, run by
the brush-pile where she and her piggies were nesting—grab
one by the hind leg, loop around the big metal feeder, jump
over the fence, come on around the truck, drop the piggy into
the bed, rest a second, step back into the pen, loop around the
feeder, grab another piggy and on and on until he had the
twelve piggies.

Then he and Alan could crawl into the pickup bed, work
them, and throw them back to Big Pinky.

The strategy operated superbly for eleven piggies. Rickey
stepped in, grabbed a piggy by the hind leg, ran for the fence
with it squealing "awheee! awheee! awheee!" and all three
hundred and fifty pounds of Big Pinky woof-woofing a few
inches behind him as she chased him to the hot wire where he
jumped and she stopped. Then she spun around and raced
back to her nest to settle down with the remaining piggies.
He deposited the piggy he'd abducted into the truck with
Alan.

With sweat running down his face, Rickey rested a moment

before he stepped over the fence and ran by the nest to grab the last piggy—a gilt. When he did, it commenced squealing "AWHEEE! AWHEEE! AWHEEEEEE!" which brought Big Pinky grunting "WOOF-WOOF" after him again.

The squealing of this piggy seemed louder, and Big Pinky's woof-woofing seemed more determined, but he said to himself, I've made it before. I'll make it again. I'll loop around this feeder, jump the fence, and drop it in the truck.

But in her next move, Big Pinky demonstrated the craftiness pigs are noted for.

Rickey did loop around the feeder holding the AWHEEE! AWHEEE! AWHEEEING! piggy in his hand. He stopped, though, when he saw he was nose to nose with Big Pinky! She'd looped around the feeder in the opposite direction.

She'd cut him off at the pass! Her curled lips, menacing tusks, and growly woof-woofing told him she wanted her piggies back.

Rickey threw the one squealing piggy at her and took off in the opposite direction.

He was moving toward the ditch the spring-fed branch had made through the middle of the hog pen to get to safety, but he wasn't moving fast enough.

Big Pinky, considering the return of one piggy insufficient, sprang after him and closed her jaws on Rickey's left bun. Pain and fear exploded in him.

He knew the likelihood of her getting him down and ripping the meat from his bones was very good. He wanted to yell for help, but no one except six-year old Alan was close enough to hear him—he couldn't endanger his life.

Big Pinky was yanking on him. She was biting down harder, too. Pain was searing through his hips, his legs. His forward motion stopped. But the terror of going down and being torn to pieces gave him a surge of energy that sprang him forward out of her jaws.

He got to the ditch where he slipped on a wet rock, twisting his ankle. He fell full length into the shallow stream.

Big Pinky wasn't a micro-second behind him. He felt her nose snuffling along his blue jeans for a place to crunch into when suddenly, from loneliness, fear, hunger—Rickey never knew why and never cared, he simply praised the Lord—that last piggy let out an "AWHEEE! AWHEEE! AWHEEE!" that Big Pinky couldn't ignore. She spun around to investigate, giving Rickey time to hobble to the far side of the pen and drag himself over the fence.

"Did she bite you, Uncle Rickey?" Alan called from the truck bed.

"Yea, a little, " he replied, wiping the sweat from his face with his handkerchief.

Sure enough, six weeks later the buyer at the sale barn did dock him for that last gilt with the uncut tusks and tail that he never worked.

But Rickey, with a cantaloupe-sized scar on his bun, flashed his amiable grin and said, "In hindsight, I know it was worth it."

CHAPTER 10

THE DAY QUETTA QUIT COWING

My younger sister, Quetta, never had confidence around cows. She didn't like to, but being the nice person that she is, she would help me with the cows if I pleaded with her. On her fourteenth birthday, I was busy. First, I had to go to the co-op for feed. Then I had a lot of other chores to do. I begged her to move a herd of Brahmans to another  field. They were unhappy where they were. It hadn't rained and they'd chewed the grass down to the roots. They'd be taking off for greener fields if someone didn't do something. She said she would.

As I walked to the pickup, I watched her edge into the field and position herself timidly by our board fence. She was studying out the best way to make her move.

I noticed the herd had stopped grazing. The Brahmans were shaking their heads at her. Oh no, I thought and started running to save her. Before I could get to her one of the calves that weighed around five hundred pounds charged over to her, reared up and knocked her backwards onto the fence. I heard her scream as the fence caved in with her lying on top of it. The calf walked over her and on down the road.

I heard her crying as I ran to her to help her up. She was bruised all over but not seriously hurt. I tried to make her feel better by telling her all I knew about handling the Brahmans then and there. I made clear to her she needn't be afraid. This misfortune didn't have to happen ever again. It didn't have to be that all a cow had to do after this would be to look at her and she'd be gone.

I told her not to let Brahmans learn they could run over her. I told her not to be quiet around them. Holler at them. Keep them moving. They'd sull up if she let them stop moving. Once they sulled up, forget moving them. Leave them alone or they'd charge her. When the Brahmans say it's over with, it's over with.

I told her all the Brahmans were that way except the bulls would sometimes paw a little bit before they sulled up. I warned her never go near a Brahman bull after he'd done that or he'd get her.

I also warned her if a bull backed up in a corner and shook his head at her, not to try to move him. I reminded her that the man who sold the Brahmans to us told us that to begin with. He said when they are backed into a corner and shake their head or look mean, that's as far as you can go with them.

The man said Brahmans are kind of funny cattle. If you try to herd them peacefully, they don't group up and follow each other like other cows. Usually, they scatter. One goes one way and one goes another. But if you go to the field taking on like you were an idiot, they'd herd up and go to the barn where you wanted them. I told her to try it. It would beat all she ever saw. It would make her feel good about the Brahmans again — like she had control over them.

I hugged Quetta and told her to quit worrying. Get back in the field and holler and stomp. Work the Brahmans by acting like an idiot. Get them moving. It would be easy. Trying to make her feel hopeful, I told her our dad, Jimmy Carroll Warren, planned to cut the herd back to where it would be only about one quarter Brahman soon. Then he'd add Charolais and Limousine.

Quetta asked me what they were like. I told her the Limousin were always ok, but it was true the Charolais would jump. I told her when they came, never let them get their heads up over something or they'd jump it.

Groaning, Quetta began rubbing her shoulder where the Brahman calf had stomped it. She said that's exactly what had happened to start all this. The calf got its head over her by rearing up. Then it knocked her onto the fence. Then it stepped on her her getting away.

It hadn't gotten too far. We could still see it a ways down the road grazing on the lush grass by the side of the road. I begged her to go after the calf because I had to get to the co-op before it closed. But she said sorry, I'd have to bring it in when I got back. Her cowing days were over.

CHAPTER 11

PINEY CREEK

Everyone knows living on a farm is idyllic: Troubles disappear in an ocean of serenity, solitude, freedom, meaning...

Nell and Jessie Womack considered buying a farm the fulfillment of a dream. With three children — Kathy, Jessilyn, and Jonathan — they moved from Dallas, Texas, where so much bad happened, to Ford Mountain, Arkansas, where they felt an easiness about themselves, a relaxation and comfort they'd never experienced before.

They bought a 415-acre farm in the isolated valley across Piney Creek. To their delight, their address became Rural Route Jim-Sams, Beyond the Boonies, USA.

The farm had an old derelict of a house—the doors and windows were missing. They intended to fix it up and live in it until they could afford to build a new one. Jessie took a job as a carpenter until the farm began to produce. Nell stayed home with the children.

In the beginning Nell spent her time cleaning out the old house. It was hip deep in wine bottles. She didn't understand why the wine-hounds who guzzled the fermented grape juice saved their bottles. Was that the only mark they planned to make on life?

One gray overcast day in late August when Jessie was in

town working and the kids were at school, Nell worked in the humid 100-degree heat that comes before a storm. She cleaned out two pickup loads of wine bottles. She hauled them to an improvised dump.

Finished with cleaning, she drove the old truck to get the mail. The mail box that went with the place waited on a cedar post half a mile up the mountain. They needed a new one. Hunters had twisted the flag off this one and shot it through the middle several times. Why, Nell wondered. Mail boxes don't bleed.

Three large men with long greasy hair and dirty clothes sat crowded together in a pickup which they'd parked in front of her mailbox. There were two empty wine bottles lying in the road beside the truck. They looked out the rear window. She saw their scraggly mustaches and leering eyes.

Oh no, she said to herself, they've seen me. Knowing she couldn't leave, she prayed, *Lord, deliver me from evil,* as she climbed out of her truck to grab her mail.

"I know you," said the stranger in the driver's seat as she approached her mailbox.

"You don't know me, " she replied.

"Yes," he said in a loud, unsteady voice, trying to point at her house below, "I used to live there."

"Did you all live there?" Nell asked, hoping to get them engaged in an account of themselves.

"Oh, I mean we drank down there," the stranger said. "Would you like a little drink?"

"Why no, I wouldn't."

The stranger reached for her with a dirty hand. The other two smirked at her with crooked teeth.

When she stepped back, the stranger said, "You furriners think you can come here and keep us from getting on a place we've been going to all our lives. What makes you think you can do that?"

"Well, our deed to it," she replied in a humorous manner. They didn't laugh. Their gravity scared Nell.

The serenity, the solitude, the freedom, the meaning of farm life — the whole reason she and Jessie and the kids had come here — had turned against her. There was no one for miles. If these men attacked her and she screamed — nobody would hear.

She knew even if she made it to the house, she couldn't barricade herself in because she'd only put make-do sheets of plastic where the windows and doors should have been to keep the rain out. She fixed the plastic so anybody could roll it up and down from either side. It would be the only thing between her and three slobbering drunks.

The men were opening their pickup doors. The one who'd been talking got out. Nell didn't know what he had in mind. I must be looking good to him she thought. And there's two more of them. How can I protect myself from three of them. Then she remembered the shotgun.

In the truck she had an old easy-to-shoot .410 for copperheads. She'd killed many of them.

She dashed back to jump in her truck and lock the door and roll the windows up. The driver of the other truck staggered over to try to open it. Nell raised up her old gun. He stepped back. She started her truck and took off for home.

She forded Piney Creek and, looking over her shoulder, hustled into the house.

Pulling the green arm chair closer to the living room window, she hunkered down behind it. Nell listened and waited.

She didn't hear anything. She looked around wondering if the men left their truck to sneak up on the house on foot. Terrified, she imagined they were bursting through the plastic door to get her.

She heard a motor. Crawling on the floor from window to window, she tried to locate which direction it was coming from. She was holding the shotgun poised, ready to shoot.

The noise grew louder. The vehicle was coming down the other side of the valley. Oh no, she thought. They've circled around to come at me from the back way.

She crawled to the bed in the bedroom where she could see out the back. She saw a haze of dust trailing down the mountain road toward her. She put the .410 in the window and aimed it. She heard the vehicle slow down.

Is it somebody lost; is it somebody coming through; is it them, Nell wondered as she looked down the barrel of the shot gun. It was aimed where she figured they'd stop.

She heard the car, the truck, whatever it was creeping along toward her. She couldn't tell exactly because of the trees lining the road.

Suddenly a pickup appeared. Nell located the windshield in her sights. There was only one man in it! The pickup was white! It was Jessie!

With a rush of grateful tears streaming down her cheeks, Nell laid down the shotgun. She ran to hug him and tell him what happened and thank God for him and here came those three drunks.

Jessie told her to go inside. He'd handle it.

Nell, knowing he knew how to deal with things like this without stirring up more trouble, did what he said.

The predators, upon seeing him, made a U-turn and barreled up the mountain. Jessie copied down their license number. He and Nell drove to see the sheriff in Berryville, who recognized it immediately.

He said the three were local winos capable of most anything.

Nell, nervous and watchful for a long time, expected the men to return and cause trouble, but they never did.

CHAPTER 12

BOTTLE CALVES

Driving along Barley's Ridge at the top of Ford Mountain, you can see Hairless Greenhaw Horsey's old house on the rim of Scrub Holler.

Scrub Holler is more than one holler. It's a ninety acre maze of Arkansas hollers connected by granite and sandstone ridges. Hairless heired Scrub Holler from his dad who'd bought it for five cents an acre during the Great Depression thinking it was full of valuable Indian artifacts.

Nobody found any valuable artifacts, and besides scrub oak, horse nettle, curly dock, and briars, Scrub Holler don't grow squat.

Productive farms with rows of chicken houses and flat, green pastures full of milk cows surround Hairless' Scrub

Holler farm. Hairless aches to be a rich farmer, not a poor one who can't even pay attention.

One morning as he was looking at his neighbors' cows, it occurred to him that valuable calves were available on Ford Mountain.

Hairless knew people repeated rumors saying farmers raising calves on the bottle attracted poverty. Figuring rich farmers started those rumors to keep him poor, he decided to fight back by buying unweaned calves, bottle feeding them, and selling them for a profit. He could then stand up and be counted. With the tiny patch of grass around his trailer full of unweaned calves, he'd be Scrub Holler Horsey no more. He'd be Mr. Bottle Feeder.

Early one morning, he took his wife's Updo's hand and headed west to Half-Pouch Disheroon's place to buy some calves and get started.

Half Pouch had the biggest dairy on Ford Mountain. He and his wife Dessie, with a bottle in each hand, were standing in a sea of bawling Holstein calves when the Horseys arrived. Hairless asked, "Half Pouch, you got any calves for sale?"

"All of 'em!"

"You wantin' out of bottle feeding, Half Pouch?"

"Naw! Bottle feeding is where life's at!"

"How much you want?"

"Cheap today...four hunert each..."

"Half Pouch," Dessie said, cuffing him, "what do you mean bottle feeding is where life's at? What do you mean four hunert dollars each? This is our neighbor! Tell the Scrub

Holler Horseys the truth. Tell them to stay away from bottle feeding calves."

"You don't think Hairless should?..." Updo began.

Interrupting, Hairless said, "I see using our yard for a pen and buying calves to fill it! I see myself raising them, selling them, and getting an easy check! I see myself buying replacements..."

"Atta boy, Scrub Holler!" Half Pouch cheered.

"I think you ought to study it awhile," Dessie said.

"Hairless! You heard her," Updo said. "We can't let a calf come on our place until we talk to Clarise Carr."

"Clarise," Updo said, when they arrived at her and Jimmy's place at the bottom of the Mountain, "you bottle fed calves for years. What do you think of it?"

Clarise

I grew up a rural Baptist in North Carolina. People didn't talk about breeding cows. We had row crops: cotton, tobacco, corn. No cows. No calves.

Soon after Jimmy and I married, he brought me here to his grade A dairy. We had fifty milking Holsteins without a bull. We had them artificially inseminated by a man named Mr. Coffee. It was my job to call him when a cow needed him.

The time I dreaded came. Jimmy told me we had a cow in you know what. I can't repeat it. I've never said a word like that in my life, and I was supposed to dial the number of the artificial inseminator!

"Hello, Mr. Coffee, my husband, Jimmy, asked me to call. He said to tell you one of our cows needs your attention," I said, when he answered.

"Why? Is she in heat?" he asked.

"Oh, my goodness!"

"Is she mounting cows? Are other cows mounting her?"

"Oh, my goodness!"

"Is she standing when other cows mount her?" he asked.

"Oh, my goodness!"

"Can you see her from where you are?" he asked.

"I can see her from the window," I whispered.

"Go look. See if there's any mounting going on," he said.

"Oh, my goodness!"

Setting the phone down, I went to look.

"I think...I don't know..." I said, when I came back, happy he couldn't see my red face.

"Go back and look. It's impor-tant. There's only a certain period of time in which insemination will work. If I come there and she's not ready, my trip is wasted."

"I'll try," I said.

"Yes, look closely."

I came back in a minute and said, "There's a big crowd of cows around her. They're trying..."

"Trying what?" Mr. Coffee asked.

"Come quick! She...she...needs you!" I said, hanging up.

In a while, I heard him turn off County Road 76—the Indian Creek Road—that passes our place. He drove down our long lane in his little Volkswagen. I went outside to greet him. He was an older person, short and stocky and balding. He was wearing boots and jeans and an old cap. He looked to be in his fifties.

I was in my young, innocent twenties. I couldn't look him in the eye because we'd had this intimate conversation, you see. I wasn't brought up to say words like he used: "Mounting, standing, heat, cycles, semen." Yes, he used all those words.

He asked where the cow was as he came closer. I pointed in her direction. I couldn't take him there. He tended to the cow by himself and left.

Jimmy asked me to call Mr. Coffee once or twice a week after that. It took me long time, but I got so I could talk to him. I told him all kinds of things, even though there was a big difference in the way we said things. I'd never been around people who talked about cattle like he did.

Breeding cows was a matter of fact for him. He was older. He'd been doing the artificial insemination for a long time. It was his job. In North Carolina people didn't say 'pregnant', and here Mr. Coffee was asking me, "Is she standing? Is she mounting?"

I got initiated into cattle breeding through Mr. Coffee, the artificial inseminator. He's dead now. He was from south of Berryville. I'm not sure, but I think he died in his pasture looking after his cattle.

Mr. Coffee was a dear person. Lots of people loved him. He was a happy, jolly person-so nice, and he and I had this telephone relationship. It was my love affair!

The calves we got from his services were good. We used the females for replacement heifers and sold the bull calves as steers if we could catch them and hold them long enough to alter them. In those days, the sale barn docked you for bull calves.

Besides calling Mr. Coffee, I had to herd our cows to the barn at sunrise.

In the spring, I didn't dress before I went for them. I just left my nightie on. I wasn't worried. There wasn't any traffic on the road that early.

One morning, I discovered a calf had gotten out. As I ducked through the barbed wire fence to get it—I was pregnant, by the way—I heard a pickup coming. Not wanting whoever was in the truck to see me in my nightie, I reversed myself to hide behind a nearby clump of sassafras sprouts. Oops! My nightie got hung on a barbed wire!

I was bent over, trying to unhook my nightie by moving back and forth, but it wouldn't unhook. I was in plain sight, hung on that barbed wire and a pickup was coming! Panicking, I tore my nightie free and dove into the clump of sprouts.

The calf stepped through the fence to join me while I was hiding in the sprouts in my torn nightie. It followed me and the cows to the barn.

Another morning, I found a cow had broken through the fence and gotten over on Indian Creek to eat greener grass.

She took off as I approached her. I ran after her through briars, cockle burrs, and beggar's lice growing along the creek and chased her back to the road.

With me following her in another ruined nightie, she walked calmly down the long lane to our house. She stopped at the gate to the barn lot. I eased by her to open it and found Jimmy had tied it with a knot I couldn't untie.

The cow went back to the greener grass beside the creek while I worked on that knot. I felt dead tired. I couldn't go after her again. Besides, it was time to cook breakfast and go to town to teach school.

Cows were bellowing in the barn lot as I walked to the house. Jimmy would have helped me with the cow if he could have, but he was milking. Then he had to go to the vet and the co-op on business when he finished milking that morning. I think the cow spent the day on the creek.

Just as sure as death and taxes, an animal will get out while your husband is gone or too busy to help; and another thing, if a cow's going to get sick, it'll be on Christmas. Cows don't know when it's Christmas!

We didn't have the ideal place to feed them. We didn't have the luxury of independent pens. We had them in a corral made of planks, in a bunch. I climbed in and out of it, carrying a crate of bottles, milk powder, and a bucket. If I'd opened the gate, the calves would have run over me getting out.

They got slobbers all over my legs nursing on them as I climbed up and down the inside of the corral. I tried to kick them away, but it didn't do any good.

I kept calves that needed special treatment in a shed. They didn't run with the others. I fed them when I got through feeding the regular bunch.

The most calves I ever bottle fed at a time was sixteen. I bottle fed three of them at a time. I put one bottle in my left hand, one in my right hand, and one between my legs. I'd notice which  three I was feeding as they nursed, beat them back when they were done, and feed three more; beat those back and feed three more...

Sometimes, one of the calves nursed a nipple so hard it came off the bottle and the milk poured out on the ground.

I had to remember which calves I'd fed. If I forgot and fed one twice, it would get the scours. We didn't have them ear tagged, so at first, I tried remembering which ones I'd fed by their faces. They get milk mixed with slobber all over their faces when they nurse from a bottle. I'd notice which ones had slobber on them and not feed them again—so I thought.

The problem was: Calves that nursed on the ears of the calves nursing the bottles and the calves nursing on my legs got slobbers on their face, too. They looked like they'd nursed a bottle when they hadn't. I dropped the slobber technique because some calves never got a bottle. I began remembering which calves I'd fed by noticing the marks on their bodies.

I bottle fed calves twice a day for many years. I think members of congress, federal judges, and everybody in the IRS should bottle feed calves. They need to get in touch with how honest money is made.

I bottle fed each group of calves for eight weeks. By then they'd be eating a pound and a half of grain twice a day and drinking enough water to make it on their own. I put grain out for them from day one. They slowly develop an appetite for it.

I had nine bottles I carried in a crate. When it was time to feed, I put milk powder in each bottle, added warm water, and shook the bottle. When the calves emptied that set of bottles, I washed them out and remade them for the next group of calves.

We had a hot water tank in the barn. I used hot water and soap to clean each bottle. I had a bottle brush to get the caked milk powder out of the bottom of the bottles, too.

You have to watch out for pneumonia in the winter, but the scours is bottle calves' worst enemy. Controlling the scours is a biggie. Calves get the scours in the summer. They get the scours in the winter. Actually, they get the scours any-time. Don't feed the calves too much and keep the nipples of the bottles clean. That slows the scours down some.

Stress causes scours, too. Your calves will be under less stress if you buy them in the early spring and get them weaned before the hot weather sets in, or buy them in the early fall and get them weaned before the cold weather starts.

We didn't get rich feeding calves, but we might have if it hadn't been for sunk cost. The sunk cost got us. We sunk money into milk replacement, we sunk money into vet bills, we sunk money into medicine, we sunk all our vacation time...we couldn't take one. I sunk my housework time, my sleeping time...

"But," Clarise said, looking off into the April sky. "I still love calves someone else bottle feeds. Oh, I'd probably bottle feed one day a month for someone who needed me."

"If a truck loaded with unweaned calves stopped here and

the driver told you that you could have them if you bottle fed them, what would you say?" Updo asked.

"Keep on rolling!"

As Hairless drove up the mountain toward home, Updo was

looking out the side window at the rose colored sky. "Clarise warned us about 'sunk' costs and calves getting sickness. I think you should stay away from bottle feeding, Hairless."

Hairless turned onto Barns Ridge without replying. His neighbors' flat, fertile farm land stretched in front of him. How different their farms were from his own small patch of grass on the edge of a holler full of ledge rock, scrub trees, and briars.

Updo said, "Stop at Betty and David Andersons'. We need to discuss calves with them."

Hairless swerved into Andersons' and parked near a row of roofed calf pens with fenced cement runways. Calves were bawling up a storm. The Andersons' van came across the field to stop beside them. Betty and David got out.

"Betty," Updo asked, "how's the bottle feeding business?"

Updo saw Betty's lips moving. She cupped her hand behind her ear and yelled, "What? I can't hear you."

"I said, 'The more it sounds like a sale barn around here, the better I like it.'"

"Can Hairless make money bottle feeding?" Updo yelled.

"Sure," Betty yelled, "if he can figure out how to get money coming in faster than the bills take it away."

"How many calves should he start with?"

"I got nineteen bottle calves," Betty yelled.

"Should he get into bottle feeding, Betty?" Updo asked. "That's what I really want to know."

"Let's get away from this bawling and I'll tell you," Betty said, motioning for them to follow her.

Betty

The chicken plant was sending us a new batch of chickens the morning I'm talking about. Well, before they got here, Dessie called to say Half Pouch was selling calves. We raced over there and bought three.

We forgot the cattle trailer. Since we were in a rush to be here when the chickens came, David said, "Load the calves into the van."

I helped him with two before sweat dripped off me so bad I sat down in the front seat. I left the door open to let the air cool me.

David loaded the third calf by himself. As he was closing the back of the van, that booger bawled, kicked him in the chest, and jumped over the seat on me. I pushed it off, and it took off across the barnyard. David and I chased after it. With the help of Dessie and Half Pouch we got it stuffed back in the van.

I walked around to the front of the van to get in so we could go and found that little bitty wiley ol' outfit already there—its back legs in the seat, its front legs on the dashboard. It was just a pawing and a kicking and a carrying on, trying to go through the windshield!

David wrestled it into the back of the van. We were rushing home when that booger began stirring up the other calves. David stopped to crawl over the seat to control them, leaving me to drive. We got them home and put them in a pen, but that booger jumped out.

We chased it all over this place! It was being such a booger I just named it Booger. It covered our forty acres here, crashed through the fence, and run plumb to the other side of Tommy Ferguson's forty, across the road from us. Tommy was cutting hay. He stopped to get down and grab it, he thought, but he couldn't catch ol' Booger either.

After he missed it with a third flying tackle, Tommy hollered, "I didn't think bottle calves acted this way!"

"This one ain't a bottle calf yet. I ain't got that close to give it one. I got it over at Disheroons' right off its momma," I said.

We rested a minute before we chased Booger all over Tommy's forty acres some more. Another neighbor, Billy Peden, coming from Oak Grove, saw Booger and headed him back to our place.

Ol' Booger romped to the end of Tommy's field, rammed through the fence, re-crossed the road, and made it to our field where he belonged, but he didn't stop. Booger crossed the field, jumped the cattle guard, and took off down the road heading west.

David and I took out after him in the van. I was driving. David had the passenger door half open. As I pulled beside the calf, David jumped and wrestle him down.

We put a halter on him when we got Booger back to our place. I mean we tied him in a pen by himself—imagine, a baby calf causing all that!

I had to get in and really nub him up before he'd eat. He was the wiliest Holstein calf I ever seen. He was a Booger.

You'd think David and I—two grown people—could handle a baby calf by ourselves without having to have neighbors help us.

Then last week, David brought a month old bull calf home from the sale barn. He put him in one of the pens and went to tend the chickens. It was early in the evening, and our oldest boy John was planning to go to a ball game. I asked him to take a minute to ear tag, worm, and castrate the new calf before he left while I bottle fed the other calves. His friend Tommy Cisco said he'd help.

The two boys are tall and stout. They took a bucket with the tools and the wormer in it and got in the pen. The first rattle out of the box, John snatched one of the calf's back legs, and that little calf drug him along like a trailer.

Tommy lunged for the calf, knocking John down, but he caught a leg. He and John lay on the runway holding on to that leg. Before they could waller it over on its back, the calf bucked around and kicked John, barking the hide off his shin and getting free as a bird.

John got up—mad. He grabbed the calf's ear and flung it to the cement. Tommy lay down on top of it. John reached for the ear-tagger, and that calf started bucking and kicking—I mean it was legs everywhere! It got out from under them, leaving those boys lay there watching it high tail it to the end of the runway.

The boys got up. With arms outstretched, they drove the calf into a corner of the pen where they wrestled it down. As it lay there catching its breath, John ear tagged and wormed it.

Tommy kept holding the calf down while John whipped out his knife to make it into a steer. The calf started kicking wildly and caught John in the chest, knocking the wind out of him. The calf kicked and bucked like it was at a rodeo while John caught his breath, but Tommy held on.

One of the calf's kicks caught John on his sore shin, making him madder. He and Tommy repositioned themselves so the calf couldn't move. John made it into a steer quick, and I gave the calf a bottle so they could get gone to the ball game. I told them I was sorry. I never expected that little calf to whup them around like it had.

I ought to say I wouldn't like Hairless going into bottle feeding because the more that gets into it, the harder it is to find calves, but I don't want to discourage a neighbor. So I'll say if he wants to put his life and then some into bottle feeding calves, do it.

CHAPTER 13

CLEO RIDDLE ON THE DEVIL'S BACKBONE

In northwest Arkansas, about twenty-five miles east of Eureka Springs, a two-sided bluff humps up out of the rolling valleys of the Ozarks as though it rose right out of Hell. No one remembers who named it the Devil's Backbone, or when, but Cleo Riddle, who was born in 1908 about a quarter of a mile from the bluff, had no difficulty understanding why. From the first time he walked along its narrow, bony top, Cleo Riddle knew that the Devil's Backbone was the perfect place for him. He vowed to own it one day, and to live there.

It took him fifty years. His family moved to the state of Washington when he was a boy, and it was there he grew up, although he returned to Arkansas frequently on visits. He even married a girl who was born near the Devil's Backbone. While he and his wife raised four children in Washington, Cleo made a living by logging fir trees, hunting bear and cougar, and cutting people's hair.

In the spring of 1972, his children grown and his wife dead, Cleo Riddle returned to Arkansas and bought the five acres that make up the Devil's Backbone. There was nothing on the ridge then, just a rough old road that cut a sharp corner up the wide end. It was so steep Cleo had to keep a pile of large stones at the bottom to load in the back of his pickup each time he drove up it.

Now that Cleo possessed the Devil's Backbone, he began, alone, to build the house he'd dreamed of as a boy. Using a pick and shovel, he dug a cellar in the rocky ground. Next he cut cedar logs and had them finished into planks at a sawmill. With the planks, he built a two-story house, topped by cedar shingles he had cut by hand. A large fireplace held an ornate wood stove with big brass knobs on the front. There was no running water, but a well was drilled and capped; Cleo planned to hook it up later. After more than a year of solitary labor, the house Cleo had dreamed of as a boy was finished.

It burned down only six months later, on a windy day in November. An antique gun and a yellow Volkswagen Beetle were all Cleo managed to save. The house, his clothes, his money, and all the rest of his possessions were destroyed.

But his dream wasn't. With the aim of saving enough money to rebuild, Cleo started working in Bruce Campbell's barbershop in nearby Berryville. He tried living in the back of the shop, but he tired of that quickly and moved back to the Devil's Backbone, where he lived in what had been his tool shed.

For the following year, Cleo worked in the barbershop to earn money, played his fiddle at local square dances, and devised several marvelous inventions. One was a better mousetrap that looked like a minnow trap, with a narrowing wire-mesh passageway that led to a baited spring. Another was a spring-loaded fuel-tank closure that eliminated the need for a gas cap. That invention featured a tapering coil in the neck of the gas tank to prevent thieves from siphoning fuel. Cleo considered taking out patents on some of his inventions, but he never did it. Maybe the cost was too great, or maybe it was too much trouble. No one knows.

After about a year and a half of barbering, Cleo bought a second-hand house trailer, set it over the original cellar on top of the Devil's Backbone, and added a couple of rooms on the side of it. Then he surrounded the entire complex with a skinny concrete trough into which he placed a wall of upright cedar logs that he had cut and peeled. With the addition of a corrugated metal roof, he had a breezeway around the trailer, giving some protection from the sun in the summer and the wind in the winter. He also had a small garage and a place to store his firewood.

Cleo's failing health made hauling water a chore, so he decided to hook up his well, a decision that led to his most ambitious invention.

With the help of his cousin Ertie Youngblood, Cleo built a water wheel that's still known locally as "The Perpetual Motion Machine."

Ertie, a welder by trade who also accompanied Cleo's fiddling with his guitar, never saw any plans for this machine; he said it was "all in Cleo's head." It was to work in the following way: A twenty-foot tower of angle iron supported a pipe containing a sucker rod that ran from the well up to a sucker pump at the top of the tower. Beside the pump was a twelve-foot waterwheel with wooden buckets on its rim. A belt drive connected the waterwheel to the pump. As water from the pump fell into the buckets, the wheel turned, and the belt drive turned the pump to bring up more water to fall into the buckets, which were emptied into a large stock tank beneath the wheel.

After he completed the wheel, Cleo began digging a ditch in which to lay pipes to his trailer, but before he was finished, he went back to Washington state to attend a family reunion and witness the birth of a grandchild.

He never came back to the Devil's Backbone. He had a heart attack in Washington, and he died on August 29, 1977.

Now, more than eleven years later, the window panes in the trailer are broken, and the wind blows through the empty

The remains of Cleo's perpetual motion machine

rooms. Strewn about on the tall bluff are pieces of Cleo's dream, violated by weather and vandals. The dream exists now only in the memories of his remaining friends and relatives.

But the Carroll County Clerk's office still lists Cleo Riddle as the owner of the Devil's Backbone.

Cleo Riddle's cabin on Devil's Backbone

CHAPTER 14

LET THE DAYS UNFOLD

B elieve it or not, Betty Jennings is retiring from a job. She hasn't spent her life telling stories as everyone in Carroll County who knows her thought. She's worked at the Arkansas Western Gas Company where she's known as "The Archives" because she knows so many people for so many generations back. Her first day there was March 12, 1972. Her last day will be March 3, 1994—22 years.

Even though she's lived in and around Berryville most of her life, according to the saying "You're not an Ozark native unless your great-grandpa was born here," Betty isn't a native. Her great-grandfather came into this world in Iowa, and he and Betty's grandfather pioneered the town of LaMar on the Arkansas River in Southeastern Colorado in the 1800s.

Betty herself came into this world in Gillette, Wyoming, under the sign of Libra — October 28, 1928.

Betty (Dooley) Jennings

I may have seen the first light of day in Wyoming, but I was raised down Brushy Hollow, Arkansas. I know there's a sign on the road that goes to Brushy Hollow saying "Brushy Creek Road" but that sign was put there by a foreigner. For me, it will always be Brushy Hollow—we moved there when I was 5 years old.

Our place at Brushy was half way between the Brushy School and the Moore School. My folks just decided on the Moore, and I walked two and one half miles each way, whatever the weather was. Anna McKinney who was born and raised here was my teacher. She was a great one.

Joe Giles, who became a military man, several others, and I started the 1st grade at the Moore together. We'd meet and talk together and holler 'Come on! Come on!' to each other. Some of the children walked with wire wrapped around their shoes to keep the soles on. Frostbite claimed many toes and fingers in those days.

We went to school unless we were sick or the creek was too high. Since no one owned radios and telephones, we didn't have instant communication — we were more at the mercy of natural happenings than we are now.

We moved to Brushy Hollow because Daddy almost died. He had Erysipelas, a serious disease of the mucous membranes. In 1932, the doctors drilled a hole in his head to draw off fluid. They were about to give him up for dead, but Grandpa Lee, my mother's dad, had met Parker Hammonds at Lamar, Colo.

Parker told Dad he had a 40-acre place down Brushy that he'd trade for a car. Grandpa, thinking Arkansas would be healthier for Dad, traded his Ford car. Some friends from Eureka Springs lived near us in Wyoming. Coincidently, they were moving back here. They accompanied us and helped us locate.

It was 1933. My mother, Marie Dooley, who lives with me

now with good health and a cheerful spirit at 93; my father, who had grown well enough to travel; and four kids — three girls and a boy (I was the baby) made the move in a car. We were the first ones in Brushy Hollow with a car, as far as I know.

We bought a wood saw and sold wood those first years for 75 cents to $1.25 per rick.   It was during The Great Depression. Everybody was burning wood. We thought we were rich. Remember, men were hiring out for fifty cents per day.

I was the the official off-bearer for our wood-cutting oper-ation. As off-bearer, I caught the pieces of wood as they came from the saw and pitched them on the pile.

I used to walk down the Hollow to Moore Church with a group of girls. I watched the older ones who were courting take off the old shoes they were wearing and take their "bet-ter" shoes from the bushes close by where they'd hid them and join the boys.

The roads were rougher than they are now and shoes were scarce. The girls wanted to look their best.

The church at Moore was the school house. It was always too crowded for everyone to sit down. One night at a revival many couldn't even get in. Lloyd, my future husband (we married on June 11, 1950) was outside looking in the window. My mischievous sister — she's two years older than I am— winked at him. It shocked him. He climbed on his horse and galloped home!

Between 1936 and 1944, our family lived briefly in Iowa,

then we moved to California. While my folks worked inside the Lockheed Aircraft Company, I went to grade school and ran a hot dog stand outside the plant at noon. I remember having chili and cutting onions real fine and fixing up the hot dogs and selling them.

When we came back here in 1944, it was kind of a shock. There was no gas, electricity, or plumbing. I was in the 10th grade. Some of that year and all of the next two years, I drove a school bus to carry one teacher, Mildred Wadel, and a pack of kids from the Farmer community to Berryville.

A 1944, green, half-ton Chevy pickup with a tarpaulin over the back served as my bus. I don't remember how much I charged, but they all paid weekly. I do remember Jack Ruhde of Brushy Hollow charged people ten cents to take one person to Berryville and back. That will give you some idea.

By that time Mom and Pop had a Grade A dairy. We bottled both chocolate and white milk. I carried the excess milk to Kraft in ten gallon cans.

I had benches on three sides of the bed of the pickup. I'd slide the crates of bottled milk under the benches and put the 10 gallon cans of milk in the middle. After driving as far as Pregnant Bridge to pick up kids, I delivered the bottled milk to the cafés and drug stores around town and unloaded the cans onto Kraft's conveyor belt myself. Then on to school.

Having spent the day in school, on the way home with my bus loaded with kids and a teacher, I stopped at Kraft's to pick up whey for my pig Daisy. She had 13 piggies that paid for my class ring and graduation announcements. Money was scarce, but ol' Daisy came through for me.

Along with many others, Lavona (Helmlinger) Schell of Schell Drilling, her brother Derrall, Jim Warren, and my cousin Jim Fryder rode my bus. One morning during the first winter I drove, the roads were slick—it was 1945, we'd just moved from California and bought this place in the Farmer Community. I got stuck between Joe Howard's Lane and Bill Walker's farm. Joe Howard's place is the last one on the right before the Osage Bridge. A lane goes through there to Pregnant Bridge. That's the way I always went.

I got out and cut some branches to put under my wheels for traction. I got back in and tried to go. I couldn't. I didn't know why. I gave it more gas. I didn't go. My tires weren't getting caught by those branches.

I looked up into the rear view mirror suddenly and saw Jim and Derrall on either side of my truck holding it back. The rest of the kids, probably including Lavona, were holding onto it, too, and just a-laughing and giggling and carrying on at me sitting there spinning.

I can still see those kids holding my bus. No! I didn't get mad. It was funny!

And no, Grace and Bob Doss's kids didn't help my kids tear out a stairwell. I tore it out myself. I did it while Lloyd was gone. He went to the sale barn a lot. Whenever I'd catch him gone, I "improved" something. I tore cabinets off the walls; I re-did the living room; I changed the porch; I cut ventilation holes in the ceiling and openings in the roof — after awhile Lloyd got shy about leaving — but the stairwell, I tore it up because I wanted to put the pool table upstairs to make a game room.

I tied sheets together and put two kids in front to pull and two kids in back to help me push. We did that until we were played out. It didn't look like we were going to get it done until Barry Doss came on his horse to visit. I was never so glad to see anyone in my life. With his help, we got the table moved before Lloyd came home.

When Lloyd came, he went upstairs and saw the pool table and came down.

I asked him, "Aren't you going to put the stairwell back?"

"Nope, you take care of it. That's your project."

To this day, those stairs are just a skeleton. That's been since the oldest kids were eight and nine. They're in their thirties now.

Another time Lloyd was gone, after we were married, I took a drill and a key-hole saw and cut that vent near the ceiling there to circulate the heat. I cleaned up the sheet-rock dust and pushed the divan to a different angle so he wouldn't notice.

Quite a while later he looked up there and said, "What's that?"

I told him and he put a metal grate in it for me.

I'd have given some men a case of nerves, but Lloyd was always proud of what I'd done. He passed on three and a half years ago, but when he was alive, he finished up whatever project I started around here, except for those stairs.

One of my first jobs was bringing in cows. Frederick, my

older brother, gave me a penny for doing it. Mabel (Smith) Dooley, Frederick's wife, tells me that during the night he would get the penny back and give it to me again the next day and the next and the next. I didn't know he was giving me the same penny. I thought I was getting rich!

So let me tell one on him: At Brushy Hollow, Frederick was taking a bath in the old #3 tub by our pot bellied stove. It was our only heat. He got too warm on one side. Halfway standing up to turn around, he butted up to that red hot stove and fried the meat! He still has a scar you know where!

I've worked in many places. I worked at Arkansas Western Gas for the last 22 years as a clerk. Residential deposits were $10.00 when I started. Now they're $75.00. The company has grown tremendously, just as Berryville has.

Before that I worked at the First National Bank, the American National Insurance of Springfield, Mo., Beck's Five and Dime, Carroll Electric, Bohannon's Drug Store, Jim Phillip's grocery. When Braswell owned the Progress, I wrote a column named "Spotlight on a Neighbor."

I'm used to working. Mom and Pop set up a tomato factory down Brushy Hollow in the 1930's. I did the whole thing from picking to packing them.

Back then, we had a tomato factory, Bruce and Anna McKinney had one, and there was one in Metalton. We all paid 4 cents per bucket for peeled tomatoes. The buckets were wood staved and held many gallons.

Women did the peeling. The factories staggered their operations because the same women peeled for all of them. They walked a circuit carrying their babies. They had a ticket pinned to their front that was punched for each bucket they peeled.

Mostly, the factories worked five and a half days a week, but sometimes the factories quit on Friday and paid the help. On those weeks the women went to Fay Worth's Beauty Parlor. On Monday, the women showed up to work with a permanent. I never got one. I have naturally curly hair.

We canned the peeled tomatoes in tin cans that came from Mun Jackson's Supply in Berryville. He charged 50 cents for a case of empties. We got around $2.00 a case after they were packed.

Pop had his own capper and a huge staved iron basket he lowered into boiling water to cook the cans thoroughly.

I can see those shiny cans yet. After we moved to the Farmer Community, during the summer, I took excess tomatoes and green beans to Springdale in the same truck I used for a school bus. We grew beans commercially, not as a garden.

We've had many operations on this 80 acre farm. We've had a Grade A Dairy, pigs, beef, chickens, turkeys, and chickens again.

Once when we first had chickens, a possum sulled up on the roost. I took a broom handle down there and poked and poked on it, trying to get it off, but I never did. It left on its own, later. You haven't lived until you've poked on a sulled up possum.

Betty's Advice

I think there's hope for this world if the people in it turn off their TV's and eat supper together and discuss and relate and ask how's your day been to each other.

People of all times have needed to concentrate on what's inside instead of emphasizing what's out there. Today is no different.

We're rushing, rushing and our families are growing up and will soon be gone and we don't know them.

There's hope if we all realize we have our focus on out there where it belongs, and not in here. Then we can change.

We smile at strangers and give our kids what's left over — if they're lucky. Some kids don't look like they're even getting the left overs.

All of this progress is not getting us anywhere. We should value what we have and stop searching for more.

We need to love and protect our families. Before we know it the family will be split up and we will be wanting them back, but it'll be too late — they're gone.

You can't please everyone all the time. You must please yourself. You must satisfy yourself to be happy. If you're not happy with yourself, you need to change.

(Betty's retirement party will be held on Saturday, March 5, 1993, at 6:30 p.m. at the Armory. Everyone is invited. Nobody tell her. It's a surprise.)

CHAPTER 15

HAY FEVER

I live on Ford Mountain and the following material is about how very important rain is here. How we know its miracle. How we hope, sometimes, that it will stay away for a while and come again another day. And how uncertain we become if it doesn't.

That's what this report is about: rain. It's also about how we rarely receive the forty to forty-five inches of it that we need scattered through the spring and summer. It's not about Buster Q. who gave me the name "Runt" because rain has fallen on my hay to some degree or another every year I've been farming, which is all my life.

He thinks anyone who can't get hay in the barn without its being rained on has to be the runt of the litter.

Buster Q. jabs it into me regularly about the rain on my hay. You ask me why I've put up with it? Well, he's my neighbor for one thing. He lives south of me beyond Sand Rock Hollow, across Clabber Creek on top of Sheep Dog Hill. It's about five miles by the county road. Furthermore, he and his wife, Violet Bilyeu, bale my hay the third week in May every spring. He's a custom baler with so many customers he has to keep a tight schedule. No one else on Ford Mountain owns a baler. They're expensive, and besides that they're a lot of trouble. I've never felt I wanted to fool with one.

This report is not about Tweedy Krump either. He's my neighbor to the north. You go across Philpot's Creek, around Goat Mountain to Lizard Ridge. That's his place on the left. It's about two miles the way the crow flies. I assure you, this report's not about him. Why would I waste my time writing about him? Buster Q. bales his hay, too, and must tell him about my hay because Tweedy likes to jab me about how his hay never gets one drop of water on it. Tweedy and Buster Q. are buddies; they go around acting like superior people because their hay never gets rained on. I said they were my neighbors. I used to think so, but they aren't really neighbors. It's just that our properties join.

My property doesn't join Arl's country store. It's several miles east of me. Usually, I go over there when it's too hot or too cold, or when I'm tired or bored. On this one morning in August I'm going to tell you about, I didn't go over there for any of those reasons. I went to see if I could buy some hay, because starting the next day I'd be forced to commence feeding my starving cows forty to fifty bales a day until the drought was over.

It had begun the spring before. There wasn't enough rain for the grass to get growing good. By May, the skimpy fescue hardly came to my knees, and the clover had turned brown. I decided to harvest what I could, so I let Buster Q. cut my hay on the twenty first.

The hay dried good. Violet was even raking it when— guess what?— one of those drenching downpours started about noon of the twenty-third.

That rain cleared the air and everything smelled real nice after it was over, but my hay crop was ruined.

There hadn't been a rain since then that had even settled the dust. Every evening when I stood in my yard over by the martin house to inspect the skies for signs of rain, I would see my cows crossing the fields looking for something to eat. Every step they took sent a puff of dust floating up around their legs.

It's hard to describe— no, it's easy to describe; it's hard to exaggerate— the things that happen and the way people feel when it doesn't rain enough, because their lives depend on it.

I've watched my ponds go down, down, down. When they dry up, where will my animals drink? Nowhere. I'll have to sell them. I'll have to put them on the market as butcher cows, and who wants to buy an old thin animal with its ribs showing through its sides? No one.

As much as a drought hurts, though, I don't take it personally. Some folks around here do. The weather's a spiritual matter with them. They judge their relationships with God Himself by what the weather does. If it rains when they need it to, that means He's judging them correctly. He's in. But if it doesn't rain when they need it and they hear of some sinners getting a good rain a few miles away, He's out. He stays out, too, until the weather situation becomes desperate. At that point, they forgive Him and let Him back in because He's the only one who can fix it.

On this day I was talking about, it was raining when I got to Arl's store around ten o'clock. I could tell by the puddles it had been raining all morning. I wondered, Why was it raining here? There was nothing around the store but an unpaved parking lot and a couple of old catalpa trees. Why hadn't the clouds opened up over Ford Mountain?

I stood in the mud for a few long moments looking resentfully at the sky before I went inside to find—wouldn't you know?—Buster Q., Violet, and Corinne, their daughter, plus Tweedy K. They were sitting at the table eating sweet rolls and drinking pop.

Tweedy jabbed me immediately. "I don't believe this rain's falling on Ford Mountain, is it, Runt?"

I shook my head, picked up a whittling stick, and sat down on the parson's bench.

"I was by your place yesterday," Tweedy went on. "Looks to me like your corn's stunted. My grandpa used to call corn like you got june-bug corn. He called it that when it was so short the june bugs could pollinate it standing on the ground."

He paused while the Bilyeus laughed. Acting as though I hadn't heard him, I cut into the whittling stick.

"How's your tomatoes?" Tweedy asked, as if he cared. "I couldn't see them from the road."

I cut into the cedar wood again.

"Are they weedy?"

"It's not the weeds so much as the grasshoppers," I said, trying to lighten things up. "My place has gotten so dry and those hungry hoppers have gotten so thick that the other day when I left my hoe in the tomato patch and went to lunch, they had the handle eaten off by the time I got back."

Buster Q. couldn't stand it when Violet and Corinne laughed. He began giving his mini-lecture about how, basically, on Ford Mountain, we have no genuine topsoil left except, he admitted, there may be some in the river bottom land.

Violet and Corinne sobered up and listened to him politely, but neither of them answered when he ended his little discourse with "Runt's cultivating land on Ford Mountain to grow june-bug corn and weedy tomatoes—land that has no topsoil. What's funny about that?"

I didn't pay the jab any mind. Some people are gripey when it rains; some are gripey when it doesn't rain, but Buster Q.'s gripey whether it rains or not.

Things got pretty quiet while the four of them stuffed their mouths with sweet rolls and I whittled. I could hear Arl in the back stacking some sacks of feed.

Buster Q. hadn't swallowed his roll when he turned to give me another jab. "Runt, if it doesn't rain over on Ford Mountain soon, you-all'll have to resort to cannibalism to keep from starving to death. I can see it now," he said, holding his hairy arm out and running his finger across it at the shoulder. "One morning in a couple of short weeks, you'll wake up without your arm and your wife'll be lying next to you with a satisfied smile on her face. You won't have to ask where your arm went."

"Buster Quilleyburger Bilyeu! That's not nice! Callie's not like that!" Violet said, cuffing him on the back of the head. Turning to me, she said, "Oren, what you and Callie need to do is bring everyone on Ford Mountain together to pray for rain. Have a prayer meeting every night. Sometimes they work."

"That's right," Tweedy said, swallowing his sweet roll and wiping his fingers on his overalls, "but tell them not to pray too hard. They tried those prayer meetings over at Rudd that year it was so dry there were cracks in the earth about an inch wide. Those people got out and prayed hard every evening, and when the rain came, they had one giant celebration. The people went crazy. They ran around in the rain thanking God for sending it to them when they needed it the most. The rain washed what was left of their crops right into the Osage River. Then they had more problems."

"I'm not worried about floods right now," I said. "I need hay. Does anyone know where a man could buy some?"

No one said anything. Buster Q. and Tweedy looked serious. In a moment or two, Tweedy said, "I may have some hay I could let you have."

Buster Q. said, "Me, too. I may have a bale or two I could let go. How many you need, Runt?"

"Five thousand or more."

They looked at each other.

"How many can you spare, Tweedy?" Buster Q. asked.

"Maybe twenty-six, twenty-seven hundred," Tweedy said thoughtfully. "How many can you spare, Barbecue?"

"Oh," Buster Q. said, "I have thirty-one or two hundred I can maybe spare."

"How much money we talking about?" I asked.

"Since it's you," Tweedy said, "a dollar a bale."

"When can I get it?"

"I deliver," Buster Q. said. "Don't you, Tweedy?"

"Yep."

Then Violet and Corinne stood up and they all left me sitting on the parson's bench whittling and feeling lots better.

I could afford the hay Buster Q. and Tweedy had evidently stored back for an emergency. I could afford a dollar a bale. It wasn't much more money than my usual baling expense. Plus this was good hay. Buster Q.'s and Tweedy's hay never got rained on. My cows wouldn't know what to make of it.

Arl finished stacking feed. He came in and sat down. He was grinning.

"I wish I could have stayed home this morning," he said. "I like the way time slows down on a rainy morning. The rain on my tin roof sounds so soothing. I could have patted the wife on the rear and stayed in bed with her."

"I'm glad you opened up the store," I told him. "I came in here this morning and made a deal for enough good hay to last through this drought and next winter, at a price I can afford."

"Who'd you buy it from?" Arl asked suspiciously.

"Arl, it's a miracle. I must've done something right to latch onto such a windfall. I bought it from Buster Q. and Tweedy for a dollar a bale."

"Buster Q. Bilyeu and Tweedy Krump?"

I nodded.

"Oren, don't you know both those birds' hay got rained on last spring? Barbecue baled it anyway and now they're trying to sell it to some poor sucker who's in a bind. Did they offer to deliver it?"

I nodded again.

"Yeah," Arl said, "and they'll throw it in your barn some day you're not at home. Don't buy that moldy stuff, hear? It wouldn't even make good bedding."

As I said, this report is not about Buster Q. Bilyeu nor Tweedy Krump. It's about the rain.

Some of us get rain when we want it, and some of us don't, and some of us just lie about it, and anyone who'll lie about the rain will lie about anything.

Lanny Gibson's Space Shuttle

SHARE THE FUN!

To order additional copies of *The Magic of Scrub Holler,* send the following information with your check or money order to this address:

Lanny Gibson
5055 CR 422
Berryville, AR 72616

Information:

Name_____

Address_____

City_____

State_____Zip_____

_____number of copies of *The Magic of Scrub Holler*

at $12.00 each (includes postage and handling).